CLASSICS

of

A. B. Simpson

Volume 2

A. B. Simpson

Trumpet Press Edition, 2023

Copyright 2023 by Trumpet Press

Author: Simpson, Albert Benjamin
Title: Classics of A. B. Simpson: Volume 2

1. Doctrine 2. Bible Studies 3. Theology 4. Faith

ISBN: 978-1-0881-8526-1

Trumpet Press is a Member of the *Christian Indie Publishing Association* (CIPA).

Book 1:
The Fourfold Gospel

With an Introduction by
Rev. Frederic H. Senft, D.D.

Book 2:
The Gospel of Healing

Table of Contents

Book 1:

The Fourfold Gospel

Introduction 5

Chapter 1: Christ Our Saviour 7

Chapter 2: Christ Our Sanctifier 19

Chapter 3: Christ Our Healer 30

Chapter 4: Christ Our Coming Lord 42

Chapter 5: The Walk With God 57

Chapter 6: Kept 69

Book 2:

Gospel of Healing

Chapter 1: The Scriptural Foundation 79

Chapter 2: Practical Directions 90

Chapter 3: Popular Objections 101

Chapter 4: Principles of Divine Healing 114

Chapter 5: Scripture Testimonies 125

Chapter 6: Scripture Testimonies 136

Chapter 7: Scripture Testimonies 147

Chapter 8: Personal Testimony 157

Chapter 9: Testimony of the Work 169

Appendix: Christian Science, So-Called. 176

The Fourfold Gospel

Introduction by
REV. FREDERIC H. SENFT, D.D.

The title of this little volume, "The Fourfold Gospel," has been a familiar phrase to thousands of God's children during the past forty years. Not that the truths contained in the statement were unknown before, but the grouping of them in this form was given to Dr. A. B. Simpson after he had happily experienced the fulness of the Gospel in his own life.

This does not mean that the blessings of the Gospel are limited exclusively to four-Christ our Saviour, Christ our Sanctifier, Christ our Healer, and Christ our Coming Lord. In one sense it is a manifold Gospel with countless blessings and ever deeper and richer experiences of God's grace and love. "But there are four messages in the Gospel," says the author, "which sum up in a very complete way the blessings which Christ has to offer us and which it is especially important that Christians should emphasize today." These constitute four great pillars in the temple of truth.

Note the order of these great truths. First things first-Christ our Saviour. Rightly, the first has to do with the soul, lost through sin and estrangement from God, but "made nigh by the blood of Christ." It is no small thing to be saved-justified, forgiven, born again. This foundation truth needs to be reiterated in these days, when sin is minimized or explained away, and the atonement of Jesus Christ is rejected by many. The same is true of Sanctification-a word and experience misunderstood and evaded by many believers. It marks a definite and distinct crisis in the history of a soul. The unfolding of these four phases of the Gospel will be made fascinatingly clear to the reader of this book. It is well worthy of thoughtful and prayerful study, and best of all of appropriating the full-orbed message-the all-sufficient Christ for spirit, soul, and body.

Dr. Simpson proved this in his own life; otherwise, his preaching would have been in vain, the Christian and Missionary Alliance would not have come into existence, and multiplied thousands of people the world around would have been deprived of the knowledge and experience of a complete Christ. Addressing an audience in London many years ago, Dr. Simpson related the following experiences which marked three great epochs in his life: "Some twenty-seven years ago, I foundered for ten months. in the waters of despondency, and I got out of them just by believing in Jesus as my Saviour. About twelve years ago I got into another deep experience of conviction, and I got out of that by believing in Jesus as my Sanctifier. After years of teaching and waiting on Him, the Lord Jesus Christ showed me four years ago that it was His blessed will to be my complete Saviour for body as well as soul."

This exposition of *"The Four-Fold Gospel"* has had a very large circulation in past years, and in this new and attractive form we are confident it will be in great demand. Nothing better, outside of the Bible, could be put in the hands of converts. One of our evangelists in the earlier years of the work used hundreds of them in that way with marked results.

The message is simple, Scriptural, and satisfying. The Church needs it as antidote to error and apostasy, a sure remedy for failure, an answer to the cry of hungry hearts, a source of health for the body and an inspiration to complete the witness and bring back the King.

FREDERIC H. SENFT

Chapter 1

CHRIST OUR SAVIOUR

"And they cried with a loud voice, saying, salvation to our God which sitteth upon the throne, and unto the Lamb." (Rev. 7:10)

This is the cry of the ransomed around the throne when the universe is dissolving in wreck, and terror is filling the hearts of men. It is the first cry of the ransomed after they reach their home and have seen all that it means to be lost and to be saved, while the earth is reeling, and the elements are melting, and all things are quaking and trembling in the first approaches of the great catastrophe. They see behind them all the way through which the Lord has led them; down that long vista they behold the toils they have come through and the perils they have escaped, and they recognize how tenderly the grace of God has led them on and kept them safe. They see the robes and crowns that are prepared for them, and all the joy of the eternal future which is opening before them. They see all this, and then they behold Him whose hand has kept it all safely for them, and whose heart has chosen it for them. They look back upon all the past; they look forward into all the future; they look up into the face of Him to whom it was all due, and then they lift up their voices in one glad exultant cry, "Salvation to our God which sitteth upon the throne, and unto the Lamb." This is what salvation means; this is what they have believed for; this is what He died to give them. They have it all. They are saved, and the full realization of it has come home to their heart at last.

Let us look a little at what it means to be saved. It is not at all a little thing. We sometimes hear that certain Christians are only justified. It is a mighty thing to be justified. It is a glorious thing to be born again. Christ said it was greater to have one's name written in heaven than to be able to cast out devils. What does salvation mean?

I. WHAT IT SAVES US FROM

It takes away the guilt of sin. It frees us from all liability and punishment for past offences. Sin deserves punishment. Salvation takes this all away. Is it not glorious to be saved?

Salvation saves us from the wrath of God. God hates evil and must punish it somehow. The wrath of God is revealed from heaven against all unrighteousness of men. But from this salvation delivers us.

Salvation delivers us from the curse of the law. We can recall the terrors of its revealing, the lightnings and thunder that surrounded the mountain, and the terror of Israel before it was given at all. They could not bear that God should speak to them thus, and they entreated Moses, "Speak thou with us and we will hear; but let not God speak with us, lest we die." But if the giving of the law was terrible, more terrible was the breaking. It is perilous to break the law of the land. The most tender appeal of affection did not avail to save those condemned anarchists in Chicago recently. The 'hand of the law was on their throats, and to the gallows they must go. I remember the days when the assassin of President Lincoln was stalking through the land. The law would have searched the world to find him out. How terrible it must have been for him to feel that the eye of justice was looking for him, and sooner or later would surely find him! The circle narrowed and narrowed around him, till at last he was grasped in the cordon. So the cordon of law tightens around the sinner who is under its power. Salvation delivers us from this curse through Him who was made a curse for us.

It delivers us also from our evil conscience. There is always a shadow left on our hearts by sin, and a feeling of remorse. It is the black wing of the raven, and its hoarse voice is ever whispering of despair. The memory of past guilt will follow people so that after many years they tell of crimes committed, the punishment for which they escaped, but the burden never left their conscience. Sometimes it seemed to slumber for a while, and at last it sprang upon them like a lion. Salvation delivers from our evil conscience. It takes the shadow from the heart and the stinging memory of sin from the soul.

It delivers from an evil heart, which is the source of all the sin in the life. It is natural for men to sin even while they hate it. The tendency to evil is in every nature, chained to it like a body of death, so that when we would do good evil is present with us. It takes possession of the will and heart like a living death. It is offensive, it smells of the sepulchre, it is full of the poison of asps, it putrefies the whole moral being and bears it, too, down to death. Salvation frees us from its power and gives us a new nature.

It frees us from the fear of death. It takes away the sting of that last enemy, through fear of whom we would otherwise all our lifetime be subject to bondage. I remember when I was a child what a shock a funeral bell would give me. I could not bear to hear of some one being dead. The love of Christ has taken this all away. The death-bed of God's children is to them the portal of heaven.

Salvation delivers us from Satan's power and kingdom. God hath "delivered us from the power of darkness and translated us into the kingdom of His dear Son." We are saved from the ills and the serpent and the bonds of sin, and the devil is for us a conquered foe. Salvation delivers us from much sorrow and distress in life. It brings a glorious sunlight into the life and drives away those clouds of depression and gloom which overwhelm us.

Beyond all else, salvation delivers us from eternal death. We are not going down into outer darkness and the depths of woe. Christ has unlocked the fetters of the pit and saved us from endless death. We are delivered from that terrible agony which the kindest lips that ever spoke has called "the worm that dieth not and the fire that is not quenched."

These are some of the things that salvation has delivered us from. Is it not indeed glad tidings?

II. WHAT SALVATION BRINGS TO US

It brings the forgiveness of all our sins and entirely removes them. They are blotted out as completely as though we had paid all that was due for them, and they can never appear against us again.

It brings us justification in the sight of God, so that we stand before Him as righteous beings. We are accepted as though we had done everything He had commanded, and had perfectly kept the law in every particular. With one stroke of the pen He erases the account that was against us; with another stroke He puts there all the righteousness of Christ. We must take both sides of this. The spotlessness of Jesus is put to your account as if it were your own. All His obedience to the Father is yours. All His patience and gentleness are yours. Every service that He has rendered to bless others is put to your account as if you had done it all. Every good thing you can discover in Him is yours, and every evil thing in you is His. That is salvation. Is it not wonderful?

It brings us into the favor and love of God, and secures us full acceptance in the person of Jesus. He loves us as He loves His only begotten Son. The moment we are presented in the arms of Christ, we are accepted in Him. Dr. Currie, a brilliant writer connected with the Methodist Episcopal Church, has left a beautiful incident in his own life. He was the editor of one of the best journals of his church, and in many ways he was closely connected with its work. He dreamed one night, a little before his recent death, that he died and went up to the gate of heaven. There he met an angel and asked to be allowed to enter. The angel asked him who he was. He answered: "I am Dr. Currie, the editor of the Quarterly Review of the Methodist Episcopal Church." The angel answered: "I don't know you, I never heard of you before." Soon he met another angel and told 'him the same story, and received the same answer: "I don't know you." At last one of the angels said: "Let us go to the Judge and see if He will know you." He went before the throne and told the Judge about his life and the 'work he had done for the church, but received the answer from the Judge: "I don't know you at all." His heart was beginning to gather the blackness of despair, when suddenly there was One at his side with a crown of thorns upon His head, who said: "Father, I know him. I will answer for him." And instantly all the harps of heaven began to sing: "Worthy is the Lamb that was slain," and he was ushered into all the glory of the celestial world. Not all the preaching we have done, or all the service we have rendered will amount to anything there. We must be identified with the Man who wore the thorns; we must be accepted in the Beloved, and then the Father will love us even as He loves His Son. We shall stand with Him even as Christ does.

Salvation gives us a new heart. It brings to us regeneration of the soul. Every spark of life from the old polluted nature is worthless, and the divine nature is born in us as a part of our very being.

Salvation gives us grace to live day by day. A man may be pardoned and so get out of prison, and yet have no money to supply his needs. He is pardoned, yet he is starving. Salvation takes us out of prison, and provides for all our needs besides. It enables us to rejoice in the glory of God, which is "able to keep us from falling, and to present us faultless before the presence of His glory with exceeding joy."

It brings to us the help of the Holy Spirit, who is ever at our side as a gentle mother, helping our infirmities and bringing grace for every time of need.

It brings to us the care of God's providence, causing all things, to work together for our good. This is never true until we are saved; but when we are the children of God all things in earth and in heaven are on our side.

Salvation opens the way for all the blessings that follow it. It is the steppingstone to sanctification and healing, and the peace that passeth understanding. From this first gateway the prospect opens out boundlessly to all the good land we may go on to possess.

Salvation brings to us eternal life. It is, of course, only the beginning, but the heavenly, land has its portals open even here, and when we at last reach the throne and look out and see all the possibilities that yet lie before us, we shall sing with the ransomed, "Salvation to our God which sitteth upon the throne, and unto the Lamb."

III. THE PROCESS BY WHICH THESE BLESSINGS COME

They come through the mercy and grace of God. "God so loved the world that He gave His only begotten Son, that whosoever believeth in Him should not perish, but have everlasting life."

Salvation comes to us by the righteousness of Jesus Christ. He perfectly fulfilled for us every requirement of the law. Had He faltered in one temptation we could not have been saved. Think of that when you are tempted to speak a hasty word, and you almost give way for a moment. Suppose Jesus had done so, we should have been lost forever. Every moment He held steadfastly in the path of obedience, and His perfect grace and obedience are the price of your salvation.

Salvation comes to us through the death of Christ. His obedience is not enough. He must die. His crucifixion is the atonement for our sins.

Salvation comes through the resurrection of Jesus Christ from the dead, which was God's seal of His accomplished work and the pledge of our pardon.

Salvation comes through the intercession of Jesus at the right hand of the Father. He is our Great High Priest there, where He ever liveth to make intercession for us, and thus keeps us in continual acceptance.

Salvation comes through the grace of the Holy Ghost. The Spirit of God is sent down, through the intercession of Christ, to carry out in our hearts and lives His work. He keeps our feet in the way, and He will never leave His work until He has put us forever into the bosom of Jesus.

Salvation comes to us by the Gospel. It is presented to us through this message, and our refusal to accept it, or our neglect to do so, fixes irrevocably, by our own act, our eternal condition. If we are saved, we become so by accepting the Gospel, which is, therefore, called "the Gospel of your salvation."

IV. THE STEPS BY WHICH IT IS RECEIVED

Conviction of sin. We must first see our need and our danger before we can be saved. The Holy Ghost brings this to our heart and conscience. Until there is this knowledge of the need of Christ, He cannot of course be received; but when the heart is deeply impressed under a sense of sin, Christ is precious indeed.

There must be next an apprehension of Jesus as our Saviour. The soul must see Him as both able and willing to save. It will not do merely to feel and confess your guilt. What is needed is to get the eye on Jesus. So Christ says to every seeking soul, "Look! Look! Look unto Me and be saved !" "Every one which seeth the Son, and believeth on Him, may have everlasting life."

Salvation comes by repentance. There must be a turning from sin. This does not consist in mere emotional feeling, necessarily, but it does mean to have the whole will and purpose of heart turned from sin to God.

Salvation comes by coming to Jesus. The soul must not only turn away from sin. That alone will not save it. Lot's wife turned away from Sodom-but she was not in Zoar. There must be a turning to Jesus as well as a turning from sin.

Salvation comes by accepting Jesus as a Saviour. This does not mean merely crying out to Him to save, but claiming Him as the Saviour, embracing the promises He has given, and so believing that He is your personal Redeemer.

Salvation comes by believing that Christ has accepted us, and counting Him faithful who has promised. This will bring the sweetness of assurance and peace, and as we believe the promise the Spirit will seal it to the heart and witness that we are the children of God.

Salvation comes by confessing Christ as the Saviour. This is a necessary step. It is like the ratification of a deed or the celebration of a marriage, and stamps and seals our act of committal.

Salvation involves our abiding in Jesus. Having taken it for granted, once for all, that you are saved, never do the work over again. "As ye have, therefore, received Christ Jesus the Lord, so walk ye in Him."

V. THINGS THE BIBLE SAYS ABOUT SALVATION

It is called God's salvation. It was not invented by man. God alone is the author of it, and He is the only Saviour.

It is also called "your own salvation," because you yourself must appropriate it.

It is called "the common salvation," because it is free to all who will accept it.

It is called a "great salvation," because it is full and infinite in its provisions. It is large enough for all your needs.

Christ is called the "mighty to save," because no matter how weak or how wicked the sinner may be, He is able to save him to the uttermost.

It is called a near salvation. "Say not in thine heart, who shall ascend into heaven? (that is, to bring Christ down from above:) Or, who shall descend into the deep? (that is, to bring Christ again from the dead). But what saith it? The Word is nigh thee, even in thy mouth and in thy heart: that is, the Word of Faith which we preach: That if thou shalt confess with thy mouth the Lord Jesus, and shalt believe in thine heart that God hath raised Him from the dead, thou shalt be saved." We do not have to get up into some exalted state to find Christ, nor down into some profound and terrible experience, but we can find Him everywhere we are. Salvation is at our door. We can take it as we find Him very near to us. No steps were allowed to God's ancient altar, for then some poor sinner might not be able to get up to it. Jesus is on the very plane where you are this moment. You can take His salvation here now. Take Him as you are, and lie will lead you into all the experiences you need.

VI. WHY IT IS CALLED THE GOSPEL OF GOOD NEWS

Because of its value. It comes laden With blessings to him who receives it.

Because of its freedom. It may be taken without money and without price.

Because of its availableness. It is easy of access, being on the level of the worst sinner.

Because of its universality. Whosoever will may take it and live.

Because of the security of its blessings. They are given forevermore. "Verily, verily, I say unto you, he that heareth My Word, and believeth on Him that sent Me, hath everlasting life, and shall not perish."

Because of the eternity of its blessings. The sun will have burnt itself into ashes, the earth will have been destroyed by volcanic heat, the heavens will be changed When salvation has only begun. Then thousand times ten thousand years shall pass away, and we shall have only begun a little to understand what salvation means. Blessed be God for the Gospel of Christ's salvation.

VII. CONSIDERATIONS WHICH SHOULD URGE US TO TAKE AND GIVE OUT THIS SALVATION

Because of the fact that every man's salvation is hinged upon his own choice and free will. It is an awful thing to have the power to take salvation and to throw it away. And yet it is left to our choice. We are not forced to take it. We must voluntarily choose it or reject it.

Because of the tremendous responsibility to which we are held accountable for the salvation of our soul. God has put it into our hands as a jewel of inestimable value, and He will hold us to a strict account for the way we treat this precious thing. If we destroy it, how fearful will be our doom when we meet the Judge of all the earth, and hear the stern question from His lips, "Where is thy soul?"

Because of the guilt which will rest upon us for neglecting and despising the precious blood of Christ, which was shed for our salvation. To neglect it is to throw it away. He has provided a great salvation. If it is worth so much to man, if it has cost God so much to provide it, what can be thought of him who makes little of it? Jesus suffered intensely to bring it to us, and shall we stumble carelessly over it? Oh, let us be more concerned than we are, both for the salvation of our own souls and for those around us who are not saved.

Because the little word "now" is always linked with it. It must be taken now or never. The cycle of life is very narrow. We do not know how soon it will end. "Behold now is the day of salvation."

Because its issues are for eternity. The decisions there are not reversible. The soul cannot come back when once it has left the body, and have another chance to secure its salvation.

When once the Master has risen up and shut the door, the soul will find it has been left out for ever. The cry will then be, "I have lost my chance; it is too late." God's Word holds out no second chance to any human soul.

Because if salvation is missed there will be no excuse for it. Not one thing has been left undone in presenting it to men. God's best thought and Christ's best love have been given to it. All has been done that could be done. Salvation has been brought down to man's level. It has been placed where he can reach it. God has provided all the resources, even the grace, repentance and faith, if man will take them. If you lack anything, God will put His arms around you and lift you up to Him, breathing His faith into you, and carrying you Himself until you are able to walk. Salvation is brought to every sinner. If the soul is lost it is because it has neglected and defied God's love.

I am glad to bring you this salvation, but eternity will be too short to tell it all. Take it and then go out and gather others in to share it. You will receive a glorious crown, but the best of it all will be that men will be saved.

In this city there is a picture hung up in a parlor and expensively framed. It is a very simple picture. It has just one word on it. On a little bit of paper-a telegraph form-is the one word,

SAVED!

It was framed by the lady of that mansion, and is dearer to her than all her works of art. One day when the awful news came to her through the papers that the ship on which her husband had sailed was a perfect wreck, that little telegram came to her door and saved her from despair.

It came across the sea. It was the message of that rescued man by the electric wire, and it meant to two hearts all that life is worth.

Oh, let such a message go up to-day to yonder shore. The Holy Ghost will flash it hence while I am drawing the next breath. The angels will echo it over heaven, and there are dear friends there to whom it will mean as much as their own very heaven.

I have seen another short sentence in a picture, too.

It came from one who had been rescued from a ship where friends and family had all perished. Those dear little ones were in the slimy caves of the cruel sea. Those beloved faces had gone down forever, but he was saved, and from yonder shore he sent back this sad and weary message— SAVED ALONE!

So I can imagine a selfish Christian entering yonder portals. They meet him at the gates, "Where are your dear ones?" "Where are your friends?" "Where is your crown?" "Alas, I am saved alone." God help you, reader, to so receive and give, that you shall save yourself and others also.

> "Must I go, and empty handed,
> Must I thus my Saviour meet,
> Not one soul with which to greet Him,
> Lay no trophy at His feet?"

Chapter 2

CHRIST OUR SANCTIFIER

"And for their sakes I sanctify myself, that they also might be sanctified through the truth." (John 17:19)

The marginal reading of the last clause is, "That they also might be truly sanctified." This seems to imply that there is something, which passes in the world for holiness, which is not true sanctification. There are counterfeit forms of Christian life, and also defective forms, which do not represent all that the fulness of Christ is able to do for us. Sanctification is the second step in the Four-fold Gospel.

1. WHAT IT IS NOT

We will look first at what it is not. There are good elements and even holy elements in Christian character, which are not sanctification.

It is not regeneration. Sanctification is not conversion. It is a great and blessed thing to become a Christian. It is never a matter of small account. To be saved eternally is cause for eternal joy; but the soul must also enter into sanctification. They are not the same. Regeneration is the be-ginning. It is the germ of the seed, but it is not the summer fullness of the plant. The heart has not yet gained entire victory over the old elements of sin. It is sometimes overcome by them. Regeneration is like building a house and having the work done well. Sanctification is having the owner come and dwell in it and fill it with gladness, and life, and beauty. Many Christians are converted and stop there. They do not go on to the fullness of their life in Christ, and so are in danger of losing what they already possess. Germany brought in the grand truth of justification by faith through the teachings of Martin Luther, but he failed to go on to the deeper teachings of the Christian life. What was the result? Germany to-day is cold and lifeless, and the very hot-bed of rationalism and all its attendant evils.

How different it has been in England! The labors of men like Wesley, and Baxter, and Whitfield, who understood the mission of the Holy Spirit, have led the Christian life of England, and America, her offspring, into deeper and more permanent channels. You will find that the men and women who do not press on in their Christian experience to gain the fullness of their inheritance in Him, will often become cold and formal. The evil in their own heart will assert itself again and will be very likely to overcome them, and their work will bring confusion and disaster to the cause of Christ. If they escape the result, it will be as by fire. You have doubtless noticed young Christians who have seemed to be marvelously converted and filled with the love of God, but they have not entered into the deeper life of Christ, and in an evil hour they failed. They had gained a new heart, but they had neglected to get the deeper teaching and life which Christ has for all His children.

Sanctification is not morality, nor any attainments of character. There is very much that is lovely in human life which is not sanctification. A man cannot build up a good human character himself and then call it the work of God. It will not stand the strain that is sure to come upon it. Only the house that is founded upon the Rock of Ages will abide securely in the wrath of the elements.

Sanctification is not your own work; it is not a gradual attainment which you can grow into by your own efforts. If you should be able to build such a structure yourself, and add to it year after year until it was completed, would you not then stand off with a pardonable pride and look upon it as your own work? No, dear friends, you cannot grow into sanctification. You will grow after you are in it into a fuller, riper and more mature development of life in Christ, but you must take it at its commencement as a gift, not as a growth. It is an obtainment, not an attainment. You cannot sanctify yourselves. The only thing to do is to give yourself wholly to God, a voluntary sacrifice. This is intensely important. It is but a light thing to do for Him. But He must do the work of cleansing and filling.

Sanctification is not the work of death. It is strange that any one should think there could be a sanctifying influence in the dying struggle. Yet many have lived in that delusion for years. They expect that the cold sweat of that last hour and the convulsive throbbing of the sinking heart will somehow place them in the arms of their Sanctifier. This comes in some degree from the old idea that their sin is seated in the body-the old Manichaen teaching that the flesh is unholy, and if we were once rid of the body, the fleshless tenant would be free from sin and would spring at once into boundless purity. There is no sin in these bones and flesh and ligaments. If you cast off your hand you have lost no sin. If both hands are gone you are as sinful as ever. If you cut off your head and yield up your life, sin would still remain in the soul. Sin is not in the body, it is in the heart, and the soul, and the will. Divest yourself of this body of clay, and the spirit will still be left, a hard, rebellious, sinful thing. Death will not sanctify it. It is a poor time to be converted. It will be a poorer time to be sanctified.

I would not advise any one to put off their salvation to the dying hour, when the heart is oppressed and the brain clouded, and the mind has need of confidence and rest and a sense of victory to enable it to enter into His presence with fullness of joy. Nor is it a better time for the deeper work of the Holy Ghost. Sanctification should be entered into intelligently when the mind is clear. It is a deliberate act calling for the calm exercise of all the faculties working under the controlling influence of the Divine Spirit.

Sanctification is not self-perfection. We shall never become. so inherently good that there will be no possibility or temptation to sin. We shall never reach a place where we shall not need each moment to abide in Him. The instant we feel able to live without Him, there comes up a separate life within us which is not a sanctified life. The reason the exalted spirits in heaven fell from their high estate was, perhaps, because they became conscious of their own beauty, and pride arose in their hearts. They looked at themselves, and became as gods unto themselves. The moment you or I become conscious that we are strong or pure, that instant the work of disintegration begins. It has made us independent of Him, and we have separated ourselves from the life of Christ. We must be simple, empty vessels, open channels for His life to flow through. Then Christ's perfection will be made over to us. And we shall grow ever less and less in ourselves, as He becomes more and more within us.

Sanctification is not a state of emotion. It is not an ecstasy or a sensation. It resides in the will and purpose of life. It is a practical conformity of life and conduct to the will and character of God. The will must choose God. The purpose of the heart must be to yield to Him, to please and obey Him. That is the important thing, to love, to choose and to do His holy will. You cannot have that spirit in you and fail to be happy. The spirit that craves mere sensational joy has yet an unholy self-life. It must get out of that form of self and into God before it can receive much from Him.

II. WHAT SANCTIFICATION IS

Let us look at the positive side.

It is separation from sin. That is the root idea of the word. The sanctified Christian is separated from sin, from an evil world, even from his own self, and from anything that would be a separating cause between him and Christ in the new life. It does not mean that sin and Satan are to be destroyed. God does not yet bring the millennium, but He puts a line of demarcation between the sanctified soul and all that is unholy. The great trouble with Christians is they try to destroy evil. They think if sin could be really decapitated and Satan slain they would be supremely happy. It is a surprise to many of them after conversion that God still lets the devil live. He has nowhere promised that He will kill Satan, but He has promised to put a broad, deep Jordan between the Christian and sin. The only thing to do with it is to repudiate it and let it alone. There is sin enough in the world to destroy us all, if we take it in. The air is full of it, as the air in some of our Western States is full of soot from the soft coal that is burned there. It will be so to the end of time, but God means you and me, beloved, to be separated from it in our spirit.

Sanctification means also dedication to God. That is the root idea of the word also. It is separation from sin and dedication unto God. A sanctified Christian is wholly yielded to God to please Him in every particular; his first thought always is, "Thy will be done"; his one desire that he may please God and do His holy will. This is the thought expressed by the word consecration. In the Old Testament all things which were set apart to God were called sanctified, even if there had been no sin in them before. The Tabernacle was sanctified; it had never sinned, but it was dedicated to God. In the same sense all the vessels of the Tabernacle were sanctified. They were set apart to a holy use. Dear friends, God expects something more of us than simply to be separated from sin. That is only negative goodness. He expects that we shall be wholly dedicated to Him, having it the supreme wish of our heart to love and honor and please Him. Are we fulfilling His expectations in this?

Sanctification includes conformity to the likeness of God. We are to be in His image, and stamped with the impress of Jesus Christ.

Sanctification means conformity also to the will as well as the likeness of God. A sanctified Christian is submissive and obedient. He desires the Divine will above everything else in life as kinder and wiser for him than anything else can be. He is conscious that he misses something if he misses it. He knows it will promote his highest good far more than his own will, crying instinctively, "Thy will be done."

> "Thou sweet, beloved will of God,
> On thee I lay me down and rest,
> As babe upon its mother's breast."

Sanctification means love, supreme love to God and all mankind. This is the fulfilling of the law. It is the spring of all obedience, the fountain from which all right things flow. We cannot be conformed to the image of God without love, for God is Love. This is, perhaps, the strongest feature in a truly sanctified life. It clothes all the other virtues with softness and warmth. It takes the icy peaks of a cold and naked consecration and covers them with mosses and verdure. It sends bright sunlight into the heart, making everything warm and full of life, which would otherwise be cold and desolate. The savage was able to stand before his enemies and be cut to pieces with stoical firmness that disdained to cry, but his indifference was like some stony cliff. It was not the warm, tender love of the heart of Jesus, which made Him bow meekly to His painful death because it was His Father's will. It was the spontaneous, glad outflowing of His loving heart. Dear friends, if we are so filled with love to God, it will flow out to others, and we shall love our neighbors as we love ourselves.

III. THE SOURCE OF SANCTIFICATION

The heart and soul of the whole matter is seeing that Jesus is Himself our sanctification. We must not look at it merely as some great mountain peak where He is standing and which we have to climb, but between us and it there are almost inaccessible cliffs to ascend before we can stand at His side. But Jesus Himself becomes our sanctification. "For their sakes I sanctify Myself, that they also may be truly sanctified." It seems as though He was a little afraid His followers would get to looking for sanctification apart from Himself, and knowing that it could never reach them except through Him, He said, "I sanctify Myself."

He has purchased it for us. It is part of the fruit of Calvary. By one offering He hath perfected forever them that are sanctified. "By the which will we are sanctified through the offering of the body of Jesus Christ once for all."

It does not come to us by our efforts, but it is made over to us as the purchase of His death upon the cross. It is ours by the purchase of Jesus just as much as forgiveness is. You have as much right to be holy and sanctified as you have to be saved. You can go to God and claim it as your inheritance as much as you can your pardon for sin. If you do not have it you are falling short of your redemption privileges.

Sanctification is to be received as one of the free gifts God desires to bestow upon us. If it is not a gift, then it is not a part of redemption. If it is a part of redemption, then it is as free as the blood of Jesus.

It comes through the personal indwelling of Jesus. He does not put righteousness into the heart simply, but He comes there personally Himself to live. Words are weak; they, indeed, are utterly inadequate to express this thought. When we arrive at complete despair of all other ways we learn this truth. And Jesus Christ Himself comes into the heart and lives His own life there, and so becomes the sanctification of the soul. This is the meaning of the text. It is to His people that Jesus sanctifies Himself, and any who try to live a sanctified life apart from Him are not truly sanctified. They must take Jesus in as their life to be truly sanctified. That is the personal sense of divine holiness. "But of Him are ye in Christ Jesus, who of God is made unto us wisdom, and righteousness, and sanctification, and redemption." Jesus is made unto us of God wisdom. He is the true philosophy, the eternal Sophia, far above the deepest philosophy, righteousness, sanctification and redemption. So Jesus in our heart becomes our wisdom. He does not improve us, and make us something to be wondered at. But He just comes in us and lives as He did of old in His Galilean ministry.

When the tabernacle was finished the Holy Ghost came down and possessed it, and dwelt in a burning fire upon the ark of the covenant, between the cherubim. God lived there after it was dedicated to Him. So when we are dedicated to God, He comes to live in us and transfuses His life through all our being. He that came into Mary's breast, He that came down in power upon the disciples at Pentecost comes to you and me when we are fully dedicated to Him, as really as though we should see Him come fluttering down in visible form yonder upon our shoulder. He comes from yonder world to live within us as truly as though we were visibly dwelling under His shadow. God does come to dwell in the heart and live His holy life within us.

In the 36th of Ezekiel we have this promise: "I will sprinkle clean water upon you." That is forgiveness; old sins are all blotted out. "A new heart also will I give you"; that is regeneration. "I will put My Spirit within you, and cause you to walk in My statutes, and ye shall keep My judgments and do them"; ah! that is something more than regeneration and forgiveness. It is the living God come to live in the new heart. It is the Holy Spirit dwelling in the heart of flesh that God has given, so that every movement, every thought, every intention, every desire of our whole being will be prompted by the springing life of God within. It is God manifest in the flesh again. This is the only true consummation of sanctification. Thus only can man enter completely into the life of holiness. As we are thus possessed by the Holy Spirit we are made par-takers of the Divine nature. It is a sacred thing for any man or woman to enter into this relation with God. It places the humblest and most unattractive creature upon the throne with Him. If we know that

God is thus dwelling within us, we will bow before the majesty of that sacred presence. We will not dare to profane it by sin. There will be a hush upon our hearts, and we will walk with bowed heads and conscious of the jewel we carry within our hearts. Do you know what it is to have Christ thus sanctified to you, beloved? Do you know personally what it is to be wholly dedicated to Him, and to hear Him say to you, "For your sake I sanctify Myself that you may be truly sanctified"?

IV. HOW IT IS RECEIVED

We must have a Divine revelation of our own need of sanctification before we will seek to obtain it. We must see for ourselves that we are not sanctified, and that we must be sanctified if we would be happy. The first thing God does often to bring us where we will see this, is to make us thoroughly ashamed of ourselves by letting us fall into mistakes and by bringing our frailties to our notice. In these humiliating self-revealings we are able to see where we are not righteous, and we are made to learn that we cannot keep our resolutions of amendment that we make in our own strength. God has let His dear children learn this lesson all through the ages, and learn it by repeated failures, and each of us must ever learn it for himself.

We must come to see Jesus as our Sanctifier. If with one breath we cry out, "0 wretched man that I am! who shall deliver me from the body of this death?" with the next we must add, "I thank God through Jesus Christ, my Lord." We must see in Him that great Deliverer, and know that He is able to meet our every need and supply it.

We must make an entire surrender to Him in everything. We must give ourselves to Him thoroughly, definitely and unconditionally, and have it graven in the heart, as if it were written on the rocks, or painted on the sky. Cut it deeply in the annals of your recollection. Always remember that on that day and on that hour I gave myself fully to Christ and He became entirely mine.

We must believe that He receives the consecration we make. He is as earnest and as willing and as real about it as you are. Amid the hush of heaven He stoops to hear your vows, and He whispers when you have finished, "It is done. I will give to him of the fountain of the water of life freely. He that overcometh shall inherit all things."

Many people make a mistake about some of these steps. Some of them are clinging to a little of their old goodness and therefore meet with failures. Others stumble at the second step. They do not see that Jesus is their complete Sanctifier. And many cannot take the third step and make a complete surrender of everything to Him. Multitudes fail even when they have taken these steps in not being able to believe that Jesus receives them. Keep these four steps clear. "I am dead, my own life is surrendered and buried out of sight. Jesus is my Sanctifier and my all-in-all. I surrender everything into His hand for Him to do with as He thinks best. I believe He receives the dedication I make to Him. I believe He will be in me all I need in this life or in the world to come." I am certain, dear friends, when you have taken these four steps you can never be as you were before. Something has been done which can never be undone. You have become the Lord's. His presence has come into your heart; it may be like a little trickling spring upon the mountain side, but it will become great rivers of depth and power.

V. PRACTICAL STEPS--

by which this life of sanctification is lived out day by day.

We are to live a life of implicit obedience to God, doing always what He bids and being henceforth wholly under His direction.

We are to be ever hearkening diligently to His voice. We will need to listen closely, for Jesus speaks softly.

In every time of conflict or temptation or testing, we are to draw near to God and give the matter over to Him. Instead of the sweet and happy experiences you would naturally expect after such a consecration, the devil comes and tries to shake your confidence by some trial or temptation. Stand in Him and rejoice that He counts you worthy to receive such trials. If you fail, don't say it is no use to try further. The principle is right. Perhaps you tried to do the work yourself and so you failed. Stop and lay it all at His feet and start afresh, and learn to abide in Him from your very failure. Israel, after their defeat at Ai, were stronger for the next conflict. Try to live out the secret you have learned. In human art there is always stumbling at first. You can learn the principles of stenography in a very little while, a few hours perhaps, but it takes months of patient practice to become expert at it. At one of our Western meetings recently, a lady was taking verbatim reports of the addresses. She was sitting at a little table with an instrument they call a stenograph. By touching the keys of this instrument a little needle cut impressions on a paper ribbon, representing with perfect accuracy the words that were spoken. She was able to learn the principle in a few hours, but it took many more hours of quiet practice before she was so accustomed to it that she could do it easily. The moment we are consecrated to Jesus Christ we learn the secret that He is to be all-in-all to us. But when we try to practice this truth, we find that it takes time and patience to learn it thoroughly. We must learn to lean on Him. We must learn little by little how to take Him for every need. The principle is perfect. It will become absolutely unfailing in practice. Remember the secret is, "Without Me ye can do nothing." "I can do all things in Christ, who strengtheneth me."

Chapter 3

CHRIST OUR HEALER

"Himself took our infirmities and bare our sickness." (Matt. 8:17)
"Jesus Christ the same yesterday, to-day and forever." (Heb. 13:8)

1. WHAT DIVINE HEALING IS NOT

We will look at its negative side first. Wherever good is to be found a counterfeit of it also will soon appear. Any valuable coin is always imitated, and the great forger has been at work on this also. It is particularly necessary with this precious truth to guard against error.

Divine healing is not medical healing.. It does not come to us through medicines, nor is it God's especial blessing on remedies and means. It is the direct power of the Almighty hand of God Himself. "HIMSELF took our infirmities," and He is able to carry them without man's help. We have nothing to say against the use of remedies so far as those are concerned who are not ready to trust their bodies fully to the Lord. For them it is well enough to use all the help that nature and science can give, and we cheerfully admit that their remedies have some value as far as they go. There is some power in man's attempts to stop the tides of evil that sweep over a suffering world. But there comes a point in all efforts when we have to say, "Thus far shalt thou go and no further." Yet no one ought rashly to give up these human helps until they have got a better one. Unless they have been led to trust Christ entirely for something higher and stronger than their natural life, they had better stick to natural remedies. They need to be sure that God's Word distinctly presents healing for disease, and does it as definitely as it does forgiveness of sin.

Divine healing is not metaphysical healing. It is not a system of rationalism, which is taking on so many forms in the world today, like the chameleon, assuming the hue of the surrounding foliage, according to the class of people it comes in contact with. What is commonly known as mind cure or Christian Science, is one of the most familiar forms of metaphysical healing. In Chicago they call it the Science of Life, but it is practically the same thing. It puts knowledge and intellect, or the mind of man in the place of God. It is not healing by remedies, but by mental force. It is a system of false philosophy and a skeptical theology; a philosophy that is absurd and misleading, and a theology which is atheistic and infidel. The basis of it is, that the material world is not real. What seem to be facts are simply ideas. This church is only a circular idea in my brain, and you chance to have the same idea in yours, and so we call it a church; but it is not, it is only an idea. As you sit there before me you are not there in tangible form, but I have an idea of you in my brain, as sitting there. I am not here either in any physical sense, but I, too, am an idea lodged in your mind.

So the teachers of this error go on to say that there is no body. Disease, therefore, is not real because it has no basis to work on. If you accept this philosophy, the bottom will drop out of all disease. If the idea of sickness has gone from your mind, the trouble has gone. This is a frank, candid statement of the principles of this theory. It has captivated hundreds of thousands of people in this country and hundreds of thousands of dollars have been made out of it. It is the old philosophy of Hume revived again. The Bible is treated by these teachers in the same way as the body. It is a beautiful system of ideas, but they are only ideas. Genesis is a beautiful story of creation, but it is only an allegory. The New Testament contains a charming picture of Jesus Christ, but it, too, has no foundation in fact. It is the old errors that the Apostle John wrote strongly against. "Every spirit that confesseth not that Jesus Christ is come in the flesh, is not of God; and this is that spirit of Antichrist, whereof ye have heard that it should come; and even now already is it in the world." This philosophy denies that Jesus Christ has come in the flesh. It denies the reality of Christ's body; therefore, it is anti-Christian in its teaching. This is not Divine healing. There is no fellowship between the two. It is one of the delusions of science, falsely so called. It would undermine Christianity. Some of us have despised it so much that perhaps we have not guarded others against it as we should. We have felt it was so silly there could be no harm in it; but we forget how silly human nature is. The apostle tells us the wise in this world are fools with God. "He taketh the wise in their own craftiness." How truly this has been fulfilled in the case of New England! That land of colleges, the seat of American intelligence and culture, has given birth to this monstrosity. It is the most fatal infidelity. It does away entirely with the atonement, for as there is no sin there can be no redemption. I would rather be sick all my life with every form of physical torment, than be healed by such a lie.

Divine healing is not magnetic healing. It is not a mysterious current which flows into one body from another. It is a serious question whether there is such a force in nature as animal magnetism, and whether what this seems to be, is not rather an influence to which one person's mind is subject from causes within itself. Whether this is so or not, the thought or claim of such an influence is repudiated by all who act as true ministers of Divine healing. Such a one is most anxious to keep his own personality out of the consciousness of the sufferer, and hold the eye of the invalid only on Christ, that he may take his healing from Him. There is nothing to be so much feared in this work as becoming the object of attention. It is heart to heart, and soul to soul contact with the living Christ, and with Him alone, that will accomplish the result.

Divine healing is not spiritualism. It cannot be denied that Satan has a certain power over the human body. Certainly he must have if he is able to possess it with disease. And, if he has power to inflict ill health upon the body, I see no reason why he should not, if he please, open the back door and get out and leave the body well. If Satan had power to bind a woman in Christ's time for eighteen years, he had power to unbind her just as quickly. If sickness was his work then, it must surely be the same now. If he can use some persons better if they are strong and well, he will do so. Other instruments he can use better in weakness and pain. We cannot but notice the strange persistency with which people of all ages have resorted to evil power, either to appease them or enlist their help. The custom is as old as the earliest races. We find it with the wild Indian in the forest, and the equally savage African. Particularly have these wild incantations been performed for the healing of sickness, and it is said that many of them have actually resulted in the removal of the disease.

There can be no question that great multitudes of spiritualistic phenomena are real. They give positive evidence of the reality of evil spirits, and they are proofs of God's terrible forewarning, that in the last days the spirits of devils shall be upon the earth working miracles, so that, if possible, they shall deceive the very elect. God's true child will not be deluded by them. If you are deceived about this thing, look out! You may not be God's true child. I warn you as you value your true welfare, avoid this seductive snare. You will find in it some reality, but it is a dangerous power and it will submerge your Christian faith beneath its hideous waves.

Divine healing is not prayer cure. There are many Christians who greatly desire others to pray for them. If they can secure a certain quantity of prayer there will come a corresponding influence for good upon them, and if all the Christians in the world were to pray for them, they would expect to be healed. There is a general notion that there is a great deal of power in prayer which must have an effect if it can be concentrated. And if enough of it could be obtained, it would remove mountains and perhaps be able to break down God's stubborn will. This is practically what this view teaches. There is no power in prayer unless it is the prayer of God Himself. Unless you are in contact with Christ the living Healer, there is no healing. Christ's healing is by His own Divine touch. It is not prayer cure, but Christ-healing.

Divine healing is not faith cure. The term gives a wrong impression, and I am glad it has been discarded. There is danger of getting one's mind so concentrated on faith that it may come between the soul and God. You might as well expect your faith to heal you, as to attempt to drink from the handle of the chain pump with which you get fresh water, or to eat the tray upon which your dinner is brought. If you get to looking at your faith, you will lose the faith itself. It is God who heals always. The less we dwell on the prayers, the faith, or any of the means through which it comes, the more likely we will be to receive the blessing.

Divine healing is not will power. No person can grapple with his own helplessness and turn it over into strength. It is a principle of mechanics that no body can move itself. There must be some power outside of itself to do this. Archimedes said he would be able to pry up the world if he could get some power outside of it to operate on it; but he could not do it from the inside. If man is down, all the power in his own soul will not avail to lift him up. The trouble too often is in his will. He tries to take hold of himself and lift himself up. He must have some power outside of himself to lift him, or he will remain down. The will must be yielded up to Christ, and then He will work in us to will and do of His good pleasure. Then the first thought will be-how easy, how delightfully simple it is to receive the power from Him which we need. It is only touching God's hand and receiving strength from His life.

Divine healing is not defiance of God's will. It is not saying, "I will have this blessing whether He wills it or not." It is seeing that in having it we have His highest purpose for us. We will not trust for physical healing till we know it is God's will for us, then we can say, "I will it, because He wills it."

Neither is it physical immortality, but it is fullness of life until the life work is done, and then receiving our complete resurrection life at the coming of Christ.

Divine healing is not a mercenary medical profession that men adopt as they would adopt a trade or profession in order to make something out of it. If you find the mercenary idea appearing in it for a moment, discountenance and repudiate it. All the gifts of God are as free as the blood of Calvary.

II. WHAT DIVINE HEALING IS

It is the supernatural Divine power of God infused into human bodies, renewing their strength and replacing the weakness of suffering human frames by the life and power of God. It is a touch of the Divine omnipotence, and nothing short of it. It is the same power that raised Jairus' daughter from the dead or converted your soul. Is it strange that God should show such power? More power is required to regenerate a lost soul than to raise the dead. God could shiver the sepulchre and bring out the forms of those who have laid there for years with less expenditure of power than it costs Him to redeem one soul, and keep His saints steadfast unto the end.

It is founded, not on the reasoning of man, or the testimony of those who have been healed, but on the Word of God alone. All the testimony that could be gathered from the whole universe would not establish the truth of such a doctrine, if it is not to be found in the Scriptures. All the deductions of the human intellect are worthless if they are not rooted there. This truth rests on God's eternal Word, or it is merely human.

It ever recognizes the will of God, and bows to that in profound submission. A Christian who is looking for Divine healing will wait till he knows the will of God, and having learned that, he will claim it without wavering. If a sufferer is convinced that the work God gave him to do is done, and that now he is called home, then he should acquiesce in that will and lie down in those blessed arms and rest. If that conviction has come to any of you, dear friends, I would not dare to shake you out of it, if you have been led into it by God. My only thought would be to sweetly smooth your last pillow, and let you depart in peace. If, however, you think your work is not done, if you have not clear light from God that this is so, if there is a true and submissive desire in your heart to live and finish your course with joy, then He who said nearly two thousand years ago, "Ought not this woman to be loosed from this infirmity?" is the same to-day as He was then. He is saying to you in the midst of your weakness, "Ought you not to be made well?" Surely that should be enough.

It may be, however, that your sickness has been allowed to come as a discipline. You may have been holding back part of the full testimony or service Christ has called you to. I am afraid, then, you cannot be healed till that difficulty is made right. You may be in some wrong and crooked attitude. He probably will not restore you till that is adjusted. He may have called you to some service and you are holding back. There will not be healing for the body till you have yielded at this point. There are hundreds of meanings in the sicknesses that are allowed to come upon God's dear children, and He will show you what His voice is for you. "For God speaketh once, yea twice, yet man perceiveth it not. In a dream, in a vision of the night, when deep sleep falleth upon me in slumberings upon the bed, then He openeth the ears of men, and sealeth their instruction, that He may withdraw man from his purpose, and hide pride from man. He keepeth back his soul from the pit, and his life from perishing by the sword. He is chastened also with pain upon his bed, and the multitude of his bones with strong pain; so that his life abhoreth bread, and his soul dainty meat. His flesh is consumed away, that it cannot be seen; and his bones that were not seen, stick out. Yea, his soul draweth near unto the grave, and his life to the destroyers. If there be a messenger with him, and interpreter, one among a thousand, to show unto man his uprightness, then he is gracious unto him, and saith, 'Deliver him from going down to the pit: I have found a ransom. His flesh shall be fresher than a child's; he shall return to the days of his youth." That is the meaning of many of God's chastenings. There is much that He would say to men through His dealings with their bodies, and it is necessary to get their full meaning into the soul before Divine healing can be received, and kept after it has been received. It is not a cast-iron patent that works inexorably in one way always; it requires a walk that is very close with God. When the soul is thus walking in harmony and obedience to Him, the life of God can fully flow into the body. Thank God, we cannot have it and have the devil, too.

Divine healing is part of the redemption work of Jesus Christ. It is one of the things He came to bring. Its foundation stone is the cross of Calvary. "He redeemeth thy life from destruction." "Deliver him from going down to death, I have found a ransom." Surely that healing comes from Himself alone. "By His stripes we are healed." That is the redemption work of Christ. You have a right to it, beloved, for His body bore all the liability of your body on the cross. Take it and love Him better, because it came from His stripes. I love to think of that word as being in the singular number, stripe. That is the Greek meaning. His body was so beaten that it was all one stripe. There was not an inch of His flesh but was lacerated for us. There is not a fibre of your body but Christ has suffered there to redeem it.

Divine healing comes to us through the life of Jesus Christ, who rose from the dead in His own body. He has gone up to heaven with His living body. You can see Him there this morning, with hands and feet of living flesh and bones, which you could handle. He could sit with you at the table and eat today as He did of old. He is no shadowy cloud-like form, but He has flesh and bones as we have. That is our Christ, a living physical Christ, and He is able and willing to share His physical life with you, by breathing into you His strength. We are healed by the life of Christ in our body. It is a tender union with Him; nearer than the bond of connubial oneness; so near that the very life of His veins is transfused into yours. That is Divine healing.

It is the work of the Holy Spirit, quickening the body. When Christ healed the sick while He was upon earth, it was not by the Deity that dwelt in His humanity. He said, "If I cast out devils by the Spirit of God, then the Kingdom of God is come unto you." Jesus healed by the Holy Ghost. "The Spirit of the Lord is upon me, because He hath anointed me to preach the Gospel to the poor, to heal the broken hearts." The Holy Ghost is the agent, then, by which this great power is wrought. Especially should we expect to see His working in these days, because they are the days of His own Dispensation, the days in which it has been prophesied that there shall be signs and wonders. How did Samson receive his strength? When the Spirit of the Lord came upon him. Then he was able to hurl the temple into ruins and their god Dagon with it. The Spirit of God was in his flesh. So when this electric fire is running through our frame, it brings healing and strength to every fibre.

Divine healing comes by the grace of God, not through the work of man. It cannot be bought, neither can it be worked for. We cannot help God out in it. We must take it as a gift. It comes to us as pardon does, a free gift from Him.

It comes to us by faith. It is not the faith that heals. God heals, but faith receives it. We believe that God is healing before any evidence is given. It is to be believed as a present reality, and then ventured on. We are to act as if it were already true. God wants us to lean on Him, and trust Him, and then rejoice and praise Him for what He has given, with no doubt or fear.

Divine healing is in accordance with all he facts of Church history. From the time of Irenaeus down to the present century there have been repeated examples of it. It is a long array, and great multitudes of healed ones proclaim with one voice: "Jesus Christ, the same yesterday, and today, and forever." All down through the middle ages the pure Church believed this truth and taught it. The Waldenses held it as an article of their faith. The times of the early Reformers are full of it. The lives of Luther and Baxter, and Fox and Whitfield, and John Wesley, give clear and convincing testimony that they believed this truth. In later times the examples of it are numerous. Germany, Switzerland, Sweden, Norway, England and her colonies, and the mission fields of the world, have many witnesses to the healing power of Jesus. Our own land, and even our own city, are full of it.

You have many witnesses to it here in your midst. You know them, and how some of them have stood the test of publicity and of years. They are not obscure cases. Many of them are men and women who have stood in the very front of Christian work. There is every kind of character and intelligence and temperament and disposition among them. There are children among them, as well as old men. Some of them have had lofty intellects, but they have been transformed into simple children. There are all classes of disease among them-from the terrible cancer to the most disordered of nervous organisms. And He has healed them all.

Divine healing is one of the signs of the age. It is the forerunner of Christ's coming. It is God's answer to the infidelity of today. Man may try to reason it down with the force of his intellect. God meets it with this unanswerable proof of His power.

III. HOW IS JESUS OUR HEALER

Because He has bought healing for us with His stripes. It is a part of His purchased redemption on Calvary. "Surely, He hath borne our sicknesses and carried our pains."

Because it is in His risen life in us. We have healing not only from Jesus, but in Jesus. It is in His living body, and we receive it as we abide in Him and keep it only as we abide in Him.

Because He enables us to take it by becoming our power to believe. He gives the faith to trust Him if we will receive it. We have not to climb the heights to find Him, but He comes down to our helplessness and becomes our trust as well as our healing. A Chinaman was once telling the difference between Christ and Confucius and Buddha. He said: "I was down in a deep pit, half sunk in the mire and was crying for some one to help me out. As I looked up I saw a venerable, grey-haired man looking down at me. His countenance bore the marks of his pure and holy spirit. 'My son,' he said, 'this is a dreadful place.' 'Yes,' I said, 'I fell into it. Can't you help me out?' 'My son,' he said, 'I am Confucius. If you had read my books and followed what they taught, you never would have been here.' 'Yes, father,' I said, 'but can't you help me out?' As I looked up he was gone. Soon I saw another form approaching, and another man bent over me, this time with closed eyes and folded arms. He seemed to be looking into some far-off, distant place. 'My son,' he said, 'just close your eyes and fold your arms and forget all about yourself.

Get into a state of perfect rest. Don't think about anything that could disturb. Get so still that nothing can move you. Then, my child, you will be in such delicious rest as I am. 'Yes, father,' I answered, 'I'll do that when I am above ground. Can't you help me out?' But Buddha, too, was gone. I was just beginning to sink into despair when I saw another figure above me, different from the others. He was very simple, and looked just like the rest of us, but there were the marks of suffering in His face. I cried out to Him: 'Oh, Father, can you help me?' 'My child,' He said, 'what is the matter?' Before I could answer Him, He was down in the mire by my side; He folded His arms about me and lifted me up, and then He fed and rested me. When I was well, He did not say, 'Now, don't do that again,' but He said, 'We will walk on together now;' and we have been walking together until this day."

That's what Jesus Christ will do for you, beloved! He comes down to you where you are. He becomes your trust within you, and then you go on together until the resurrection light and glory of the coming age bursts in upon you. May God help us all to receive Him thus fully for His own name's sake! Amen.

Chapter 4

CHRIST OUR COMING LORD.

"I will give him the morning star." (Rev. 2:28)

The Second Coming of the Lord Jesus Christ is a distinct and important part of the Apostolic Gospel. "I declare unto you the Gospel," Paul says to the Corinthians, and then begins to tell them of the Resurrection and the Second Advent. It is, indeed, good news to all who love Him and mourn the sins and sorrows of a ruined world.

It is the glorious culmination of all other parts of the Gospel. We have spoken of the Gospel of SALVATION, but Peter says our salvation is "ready to be revealed in the last time." Then only, when we stand amid the wreck of time and secure upon the Rock of Ages,

> "Then, Lord, shall we fully know,
> Not till then, how much we owe."

We have spoken of SANCTIFICATION, but John says: "When He shall appear, we shall be like Him, and every man that hath this hope in him purifieth himself, even as He is pure." And we have spoken of DIVINE HEALING, but Paul says: "God hath given us the 'EARNEST' of the resurrection in our bodies now," and Divine healing is but the first-springing life of which the resurrection will be the full fruition.

So that the truth and hope of the Lord's coming is linked with all truth and life, and is the Church's great and blessed hope. In the very beginning of human history God placed this great hope before His children. In the hour when man fell from Paradise, God erected in that fallen Eden in the majestic figures of THE CHERUBIM, the prophecy and symbol of man's future glory. The faces of the lion, the ox, the man, and the eagle, were the types of royalty, the strength, the wisdom, and the lofty elevation to which redeemed man was to rise in Jesus. These figures run through all the dispensations. They are God's portrait of His redeemed child after redemption's work is done. God sets before Himself and before man His sublime ideal for his future, and He will never rest till it is fulfilled. It is, therefore, well that besides the Gospel for the present, we should understand, and live under the power of THE GOSPEL OF THE FUTURE and the blessed and purifying hope of Christ's glorious coming.

I. WHAT WE MEAN BY CHRIST'S COMING

We do not mean His coming to the individual Christian's heart. He does thus come most truly and graciously, and this is the blessed mystery of which we have already spoken in connection with our sanctification. It is "Christ in you, the hope of glory." But this is not His second coming. Some persons are ready to say, with a great show of spirituality, I have the millennium in my heart, and the Lord in my heart; let those who have not, speculate about a material coming. Well, Paul had the Lord in his heart, and a millennium as near to the third heaven as these persons will probably claim; and John was about as near his Redeemer's heart as any of us can ever expect to get on earth; but they did speak and write in terms like this: "Then we which are alive, and remain unto the coming of the Lord, shall be caught up in the clouds to meet the Lord in the air." "We "We know that when He shall appear, we shall appear with Him in glory." "Behold, He cometh with clouds, and every eye shall see Him. Even so, come, Lord Jesus."

Indeed, the more we know Jesus spiritually, the more will we long for His personal and eternal presence in the fuller and more glorious sense which His personal advent will bring.

We do not mean His coming at death. It is doubtful whether He does really come for us at death. Lazarus is represented as borne by angels into Abraham's bosom; and Stephen at his glorious departing saw Jesus in heaven on the right hand of God, rising, it is true, to receive and honor His faithful servants, but not coming for him personally. The contrasts between death and the Lord's coming are very marked. We are not told to watch for death, but are delivered from its fear, but we are to watch for the Lord's coming. Death is an enemy; His coming a welcome visitation of our dearest friend. Death is a bitter bereavement to the heart; the Lord's coming is the very consolation of the bereaved, and the antidote of death. If death and the Lord's coming were identical, then the apostle would have said to the Thessalonian believers: "I would not have you ignorant concerning them that are asleep, that ye sorrow not as those that have no hope, for the Lord has come for them, and will soon in like manner come for you in death, and you shall be sweetly united in death once more." Does he say that? No! But he does say: "The Lord shall DESCEND FROM HEAVEN, and THE DEAD IN CHRIST SHALL RISE first, and then we that are alive shall be caught up together with them, to meet the Lord in the air, and so we shall be ever with the Lord." It is not death he points them to, but that which is to overcome death, and of which he says in writing to the Corinthians: "Then shall be brought to pass the saying that is written, 'Death is swallowed up in victory.'" If the Lord's coming is to swallow up death in victory, it is very certain that it cannot be the same thing, or it would swallow up itself.

We do not mean the spiritual coming of Christ through the spread of the Gospel and the progress of Christianity. This is nowhere recognized in the Bible as the personal coming of Christ. "Behold, He cometh with clouds, and EVERY EYE

SHALL SEE HIM, and they also which pierced Him, and ALL KINDREDS OF THE EARTH SHALL WAIL BECAUSE OF HIM." Now, that is not the way they do when they receive the Gospel. They rejoice. But now they are startled and discouraged. And they cry, as represented in another place, to the rocks and the mountains to fall upon them and hide them from the wrath of the Lamb. So, also, the angels, speaking of this event to the eleven disciples, say: "This same Jesus SHALL SO COME IN LIKE MANNER AS YE HAVE SEEN HIM GO INTO HEAVEN." This cannot be the publication of the Gospel, but must be HIS PERSONAL, VISIBLE, AND GLORIOUS APPEARING. The Gospel is to be widely diffused; His truth is to prevail; His cause is to triumph, but He is coming personally, and He is infinitely more than even His truth and cause.

II. WHAT DO WE MEAN BY THE MILLENNIUM?

Some persons have stated that the doctrine of the millennium is a modern invention, and that the word itself is not found in the Bible.

The word millennium is not English, but is the Greek word for a thousand years. It is used repeatedly in the twentieth chapter of Revelation to denote the period during which Christ shall reign with His saints on the earth after the first resurrection. It is a time of victory, joy and glory. Seven especial facts are recorded concerning it here:

> The resurrection and re-union of the saints.
> Their reward and reign.
> The complete exclusion of Satan from the earth.
> The personal and continual presence of Jesus with them on earth.
> The suppression of all enemies and the universal reign of righteousness.
> The duration of a thousand years.

The immediately succeeding revolt of Satan and sinful man, and the final judgment of the wicked.

If there was no other reference in the Bible to this time of blessing, these elements alone would be sufficient to constitute a state and time of exalted glory and happiness. Much more do they suffice to identify it as the golden age of which former prophets wrote and spake, when righteousness, truth and peace shall "cover the earth as the waters cover the sea."

III. THE ORDER OF THESE TWO EVENTS

This is the next question to be settled, and upon it hang most of the issues of the question. Is the coming of Christ to precede or follow this millennial period?

The most obvious reason for believing that it precedes it, is found in the very passage just referred to where these events are both described. There can be no question that here the coming of the Lord precedes and introduces the millennium. His coming is minutely depicted in the whole procession from heaven to earth. Then follows the conquest and punishment of His earthly foes, the binding of Satan, the resurrection of the saints, the reign of the risen ones and the thousand years. The only way it is attempted to set this aside is to represent it as figurative and spiritual. Dean Alford's strong sense and honesty is the best answer to this. If this be so, he declares, then adieu to all definiteness and certainty in the Scriptures. If this be not a literal coming, resurrection, and millennium, then we do not know what our Bibles mean about anything.

The next argument for Christ's premillennial coming is the emphatic use of the word, "WATCH," in connection with it. Many times are we told to watch for it. Now if it is to be preceded by a spiritual millennium, the Lord would have told us to watch for this. How could the early Church watch for His coming, how can even we if we know that it is to be preceded by a clear thousand years? The very word watch means immanency, and it is not immanent, if ten whole centuries must intervene. If it be objected that as a matter of fact Christ's coming did not occur during more than ten centuries, this does not alter its immanency. An event may be liable to occur at any moment for years, and yet be long retarded. That is quite different from its being understood as not to occur until the later period. Although God knew just the moment when His Son should appear, yet He wanted His Church to be always expecting it-at even, or at midnight, or at the cock crowing, or in the morning. The announcement of a fixed previous millennium would have been fatal to this design, and the Church would have gone to work to make her own millennium without Him. This is just what the Romish Church did, when Pope Hildebrand announced in the tenth century that the millennium had begun, and that Christ was already present through His vicar. And some Protestant teachers have the assumption to tell us today that this century of progress is the first age of the millennium.

The next proof of a premillennial coming is found in the picture Christ gives us of the condition of things as they were to be down to the close of the Christian age, and up to the very hour of His coming.

Just glance at a few bold touches in the picture.

Some seed fell by the wayside and the fowls of the air devoured them; some fell on stony places and perished; some were choked by thorns, and some fell on good ground and bore fruit.

But soon the enemy sowed the tares, and both grow together till the harvest.

The Church, externally, grows up into luxuriant strength like the mustard plant, but internally is full of leaven. The true and pure are like the hid treasure and the pearl, so hard to find. The net gathers of every kind and only the angels can separate the evil at the last.

As the ages roll on, there looms up the picture, not of a millennium, but a "Falling away first." "Wickedness shall abound and the love of many shall wax cold." "Many shall depart from the faith, giving heed to doctrines of devils." "In the last days perilous times shall come." There shall be plenty of church members, "having a form of godliness"; but these shall be the very enemies of the Cross of Christ, "denying the power thereof." A holy, happy world will not be waiting to welcome its King, but "as a snare shall He come unto all that dwell on the earth." "When they shall say, 'Peace and safety, then sudden destruction.'" And when it bursts upon them, it shall find them "as it was in the days of Noah and of Lot"; and the Master even asks, "When the Son of man cometh, shall He find faith on the earth?"

This is God's picture of the future of earth until Christ's coming. It does not look much like a previous millennium.

No, nor does the story of eighteen centuries move towards a spiritual millennium. New York with half the proportion of church goers and nearly double the ratio of drunkards, has not grown any nearer to it in two hundred years; London, with three million souls who never enter a church; Berlin, with one minister to fifty thousand people; these three capitals of the three great Protestant nations of earth hold out no signal of its coming. And what shall we say of wicked Paris, and rotten Constantinople, and idolatrous India, and conservative China, and savage Africa? When is there coming to them as much millennial light as we have? When will the Christian nations begin to move toward their golden age? Oh, if this be the best God has for us, then prophecy is an exaggeration and the Bible a poetic dream. Thank God, He is coming and His Kingdom shall transcend our brightest hope, and His own most glowing picture.

IV. OBJECTIONS

The strongest objections that are made to this doctrine are:

It dishonors the work of the Holy Ghost, as if He were incompetent to fulfill His administration, and were represented as having failed in His great mission to convert the world, and some other means had had to be provided. In reply it is enough to say that the Holy Ghost has not undertaken to convert the world, but to call out of it the Church of Christ and prepare a people for His name, and when this is done, and all who will accept Jesus as a Saviour have been called, converted and fully trained, the time for the next stage will have come, and Jesus will come to reign and restore His ancient people for their privileges and opportunities. The work of the Holy Ghost will not cease then, for He shall abide with us for ever, and the ages to come shall afford unbounded and more glorious scope for His grace and power.

It is objected that such a doctrine discourages Christian missions, and saps the foundations of the Church's most glorious hopes and prospects. On the contrary, it opens a prospect of far grander glory to the Church at her Lord's appearing, and bids her go forth, rapt with the desire to hasten it, to prepare the world for His appearing; for as an incentive to this work, He Himself has told her that when the message of salvation has been proclaimed to all the world, then shall the end come. The fact is that a large majority of the missionaries now in foreign lands believe and rejoice in the blessed hope of the Lord's coming, are animated by it to labor for the world's evangelization, and cheered by the blessed thought that their task is not to convert the whole human race, but to evangelize the nations, and give every man a chance to be saved if he will; and they would, indeed, be distracted and dismayed at the prospect they behold, did they feel that the world must wait until the present agencies have wrought out its full salvation, while meanwhile three times its entire population every century is swept into eternity unsaved. The coming of Christ is not going to suspend mission work. It will bring the most glorious and complete system of evangelization earth has ever seen. And under its benignant influence the heathen shall all be brought to Jesus; all nations shall be blessed in Him, and all people shall call Him blessed. The most ardent friends of lost humanity must long the most for this, the world's best hope.

It is objected that this doctrine leads to fanaticism. Anything may be abused, but in the sober and Scriptural faith of this doctrine there is nothing fitted to minister to rashness, presumption or folly. Let us very carefully avoid all attempts to prophesy ourselves, or be wise above that which is written; but let us not be intimidated by the devil's howl, from the fullness of God's truth and testimony. This truth will make us a peculiar people. It will take away the charm of the world, and separate us from it. It will make us very unlike many selfish and comfortable Christians, and will set our soul on fire to serve God and save men. And if that be fanaticism, then welcome such fanaticism.

It is objected that it is gross and material, tending to promote earthly and carnal hopes in the heart and the Church, like the earthly ideas and ambitions of the primitive apostles which the Master rebuked, and taught them rather to look for a spiritual kingdom and a heavenly home. That was the extreme then, may not the opposite be now? Is not the true need the spiritual first, afterward the material, the resurrection life of the soul first, then the resurrection of the body? We do not hold nor teach any gross or material idea of the material idea of the millennial age. The bodies of the saints will be spiritual, and like His own. But if He was pleased to take such a body into the heavenly world and make it the center and crown of creation, is it anything but an affectation to try to be more spiritual than our Lord? Nay, it is all spiritual, and the true purpose and end of redemption is that "our whole spirit and soul and body be preserved blameless unto the coming of our Lord Jesus Christ," and "the whole earth be filled with His glory."

V. THE SIGNS OF HIS COMING

While the day and the hour shall be unrevealed, yet His children "are not in darkness that that day should overtake them as a thief." "None," as the end approaches, "none of the wicked shall understand, but the wise shall understand."

There is a distinct order revealed. He will first come for His own waiting ones, and they, with the holy dead, shall be caught up to meet Him in the air. The wicked world shall be left behind; a formal church and a multitude of nations shall live on and scarcely miss the little flock that has just been caught away. Then will begin a series of judgments and warnings, ending at last in the descent of Christ in power and glory, the revelation of His righteous judgment against His open enemies, and the beginning of His personal reign. There will thus be two appearings of Jesus Christ-the one to His own, the other, later, to the entire world; the first as a Bridegroom, the second as a King and Judge. The signs of the one do not therefore apply to the other. The first of these appearings is not so sharply defined as the other. It is more immanent and uncertain, and may come at any hour.

Many of the most important signs of the Lord's coming have already been fulfilled. *For example*:

> The political changes and developments of Daniel's great visions have apparently all occurred. The great empires have come and gone, and the minor kingdoms which were to succeed them are now covering the regions which once they swayed.
>
> The predicted "Falling away," has long ago begun, and the man of sin has sat in God's temple already the full time of the prophetic cycle, and the process has begun which is to "consume and destroy unto the end." The Papacy has fulfilled almost all the lineaments of its marvelous portrait.
>
> The Mohammedan power has waxed and waned, and the waters of this great spiritual Euphrates are being dried up every day to prepare the way of God's kingly people.
>
> The Jewish signs have not been less remarkable. Jacob is turning his face again to Bethel, and Jerusalem is preparing to put on her beautiful garments again. Her sons are slowly gathering, while jealous nations are hastening the exodus, and fulfilling unconsciously the voice of prophecy.

The intellectual signs are not less marked. Knowledge is indeed increased, and many run to and fro, while human philosophy talks of evolution and declares that all things continue as they were, and nature is immutable and only material.

The moral signs are even more marked than Daniel's picture. "The wicked shall do wickedly," was never more true than today. Portentous forms of wickedness startle the moral sense every day, and invention is as ripe in evil as it is in material art.

The religious signs are growing more vivid. Lukewarmness and worldliness in the Church, intense longings after holiness on the part of the few, and a mighty missionary movement are the features of the age, and the signs of prophecy, that point to the day of the Son of Man.

And finally, an earnest, a growing and a world-wide expectation of His coming on the part of all those who love His appearing, is as profound today as it was in Judea, and even the Gentile world in the age preceding His advent at Bethlehem. The morning star is in the East. "The children of the day" have seen it. The cry has gone forth, "The night is far spent, the day is at hand"; and soon the Sun will fill the sky and cover the earth with millennial glory.

VI. THE BLESSINGS OF HIS COMING

I. It will bring us Jesus Himself. This is the best of its blessings. Like all the other sections of this Gospel, this, too, is the Gospel of Himself. Not the robes and the royal crowns, not the resurrection bodies or reunited friends will be the chief joy, but

> "Thou art coming, we shall see Thee,
> And be like Thee on that day."

It will bring us our friends. "Them who sleep in Jesus will God bring with Him." They shall be alive, they shall be recognized, they shall be gloriously beautiful, they shall be ours forever. Not only the old ones, but such new ones, the good of all the ages, the men and women we have longed to know. What a family!

"Ten thousand times ten thousand,
In shining garments bright,
The armies of the ransomed
Throng up the steps of light;
O then, what rapturous greetings
On Canaan's happy shore,
What knitting severed friendships up,
Where partings are no more."

It will bring us perfect spirits, restored to His image, glorious in His likeness, free from fault, defect, or imperfection, removed above temptation, incapable of falling, and overflowing with unutterable blessedness. We shall wear His perfect image; we shall know as we are known; we shall be as holy as He is holy; we shall possess His strength and beauty and perfect love. The universe will gaze upon us, and next to the glory of the Lamb will be the beauty of the bride.

We shall have perfect bodies; we shall possess His perfect resurrection life; we shall forget even what a pain was like; we shall spring into boundless strength; our hearts shall thrill with the fullness of immortal life, and space and distance be annihilated. The laws of gravitation will hold us no more. The streets of the New Jerusalem vertically and horizontally, the length and breadth, and the height thereof are equal. Our bodies shall be the perfect instruments of our exalted spirits, the exact reflection of His glorious body.

It will give us the sweetest and highest service. It will be no idle, selfish ecstasy, but will bring a perfect partnership in His kingdom and administration. We shall, perhaps, be permitted to fulfill the ideals of our highest earthly experiences, and finish the work we have longed and tried to do-with boundless resources, infinite capabilities, unlimited scope and time, and His own presence and omnipotent help. The blessed work will be to serve Him, to bless others, and to raise earth and humanity to happiness, righteousness and Paradise restored.

It will banish Satan. It will bind and chain the foe and fiend, whose hate and power have held the world in ages of darkness and misery. Oh, to be free from his presence for even a day! to feel that we need no longer watch with ceaseless vigilance against him! to walk upon a world without a devil! Lord, hasten that glorious day!

And it will bring such blessings to others, to the race, to the world. It will stop the awful tragedy of sin and suffering; it will sheathe the sword, emancipate the captive, close the prison and the hospital, bind the devil and his henchman, Death; beautify and glorify the face of the earth; evangelize and convert the perishing nations, and shed light and gladness on this dark scene of woe and wickedness.

> There shall he no more crying,
> There shall be no more pain.
> There shall be no more dying,
> There shall be no more stain.
>
> Hearts that by death were riven,
> Meet in eternal love;
> Lives on the altar given
> Rise to their crowns above.
>
> Satan shall tempt us never,
> Sin shall o'ercome no more,
> Joy shall abide forever,
> Sorrow and grief be o'er.
>
> Jesus shall be our glory,
> Jesus our heaven shall be;
> Jesus shall be our story,
> Jesus who died for me.
>
> Hasten, sweet morn of gladness,
> Hasten, dear Lord, we pray;
> Finish this night of sadness,
> Hasten the heavenly day.
>
> Jesus is coming surely,
> Jesus is coming soon;
> O let us walk so purely,
> O let us keep our crown.

Jesus, our watch we are keeping,
Longing for Thee to come;
Then shall be ended our night of weeping,
Then we shall reach our home.

VII. THE LESSONS IT LEAVES

Let us be ready. "The marriage of the Lamb is come and His wife hath made herself ready, and to her it was GRANTED that she should be arrayed in fine raiment, clean and white." Thank God that the robes are given. Let us have them on. WHITE ROBES. When the Bride is dressed, the wedding must be near. So let us hasten His coming.

Let us be watching. "Behold, I come as a thief: blessed is he that watcheth and keepeth his garments, lest he walk naked and they see his shame." Let us not put off the wedding robe for an hour. Let us remember His words. "When these things begin to come to pass, then lift up your heads and bend YOURSELVES BACK (Dr. Young), for your redemption draweth nigh." Keep your faces turned heavenwards until your whole being shall curve heavenwards, like a dear, old colored saint we know, whose body, when she speaks and prays, describes a circle bending towards the sky.

Be faithful. It is to bring the reward of faithful servants. Let us "look to it that we lose none of the things which we have wrought, but may receive a full reward." "Hold fast that thou hast that no man take thy crown."

In the ancient Church there was a noble band of forty faithful soldiers in one of the Roman legions who were condemned to die for their faith in Jesus. They were all exposed on the centre of a frozen lake, to perish on the ice, but allowed the choice of recanting from their faith at any moment during the fatal night by walking to the shore and reporting to the officer on duty.

As the night wore on the sentinel on shore saw a cloud of angels hovering over the place where the martyrs stood, and as one by one they dropped, they placed a crown upon the martyr's brow and bore him up to the skies, while all the air rang with the song, "Forty Martyrs and Forty Crowns." At last they had all gone but one, and his crown still hung in the sky above and no one seemed to claim it. Suddenly the sentinel heard a step, and lo! one of the forty was at his side. He had fled. The sentinel looked at him as he took down his name, and then said: "Fool, had you seen what I have seen this night you would not have lost your crown. But it shall not be lost. Take my place, and I will gladly take yours;" and forth he marched to death and glory, while again the silent choir took up the chorus, "Forty Martyrs and Forty Crowns. Thou hast been faithful unto death and thou shalt receive a crown of life."

God help us to hear that chorus when He shall come!

Be diligent. There is much to do. You. can "hasten the coming of the day of God." The world is to be forewarned. The Church is to be prepared. Arouse thee, O Christian. Give Him every power, every faculty, every dollar, every moment. Send the Gospel abroad. Go yourself if you can. If you cannot, send your substitute. And may this last decade of the nineteenth century mean for you and for this world, as nothing ever meant before, a time of preparation for the coming of our Lord and Saviour Jesus Christ!

Chapter 5

THE WALK WITH GOD.

"He that saith he abideth in Him, ought himself so to walk even as He walked." (I John 2:6)

The life naturally leads to the walk. The term describes the course of life, the conduct, the practical side of our Christian life. The reference to the walk of our Lord Jesus Christ recalls His character and life. The character of Jesus stands out as the divinest monument of the Bible and the Gospels.

Even men who do not believe in Him as we do have been compelled to acknowledge the grandeur and loftiness of His incomparable life. Here are some of the testimonies that the world's illustrious thinkers have borne to Jesus of Nazareth. Renan says "The Christ of the Gospels is the most beautiful Incarnation of God. His beauty is eternal; His reign shall never end." Goethe says "There shines from the Gospels a sublimity through the person of Christ which only the divine could manifest." Rosseau writes "Was He no more than man? What sweetness! What purity in His ways! What tender grace in His teaching! What loftiness in His maxims! What wisdom in His words! What delicacy in His touch! What an empire in the hearts of His followers! Where is the man, where is the sage that could suffer and die without weakness or display? So grand, so inimitable is His character that the inventors of such a story would be more wonderful than the character which they portrayed." Carlyle says "Jesus Christ is the divinest Symbol.

Higher than this human thought can never go." Napoleon said "I am a man, I understand men. These were all men. Jesus Christ was more than man. Our empire is built on force, His on love, and it will last when ours has passed away."

But if Jesus Christ thus appears at a distance to the minds that can only admire Him, how much more must He be to those who know Him as a personal Friend and who see Him in the light of love, for--

> The love of Jesus, what it is,
> None but His loved ones know.

The character and life of Christ have a completeness of detail which no other Bible biography possesses. The story has been written out by many witnesses, and the portrait is reproduced in all its lineaments and features. He has traversed every stage of life from the cradle to the grave, and represented humanity in every condition and circumstance of temptation, trial and need, so that His example is equally suited to childhood, youth or manhood, to the humble and the poor, in life's lowliest path, or to the sovereign that sways the widest scepter, for He is at once the lowly Nazarene and the Lord of Lords. He has felt the throb of every human affection. He has felt the pang of every human sorrow. He is the Son of Man in the largest, broadest sense. Nay, His humanity is so complete that He represents the softer traits of womanhood as well as the virility and strength of manhood, and even the simplicity of a little child, so that there is no place in the experiences of life where we may not look back at this Pattern Life for light and help as we bring it into touch with our need and ask, "What would Jesus do?"

God has sent forth the life of Christ as our Example and commanded us to imitate and reproduce Him in our lives. This is not an ideal picture to study as we would some paragon of art. It is a life to be lived and it is adapted to all the needs of our present existence. It is a plain life for a common people to copy, a type of humanity that we can take with us into the kitchen and the family room, into the workshop and the place of business, into the field where the farmer toils, and the orchard where the gardener prunes, and the place where the tempter assails, and even the lot where want and poverty press us with their burdens and their cares. This Christ is the Christ of every man who will receive Him as a Brother and follow Him as an Example and a Master. "I have given you an example," He says, "that ye should do as I have done." He expects us to be like Him. Are we copying Him and being made conformable unto His image? There is but one Pattern. For ages God "sought for a man and found none." At last humanity produced a perfect type and since then God has been occupied in making other men according to this Pattern. He is the one original. When Judson came to America the religious papers were comparing him to Paul and the early apostles, and Judson wrote expressing his grief and displeasure and saying, "I do not want to be like them. There is but One to copy, Jesus Himself. I want to plant my feet in His footprints and measure their shortcomings by His and His alone. He is the only Copy. I want to be like Him." So let us seek to walk even as He walked.

The secret of a Christ-like life lies partly in the deep longing for it. We grow like the ideals that we admire. We reach unconsciously at last the things we aspire to. Ask God to give you a high conception of the character of Christ and an intense desire to be like Him and you will never rest until you reach your ideal. Let us look at this Ideal.

I. THE MOTIVE OF HIS LIFE

The key to any character is to be found in its supreme motive, the great end which it is pursuing, the object for which it is living. You cannot understand conduct by merely looking at facts. You want to grasp the intent that lies back of these facts and incidents, and the supreme reason that controls these actions. When a great crime has been committed the object of the detective is to establish a reason for it, then everything else can be made plain. The great object for which we are living will determine everything else, and explain many things which otherwise might seem inexplicable. When the ploughman starts out to make a straight furrow he needs two stakes. The nearer stake is not enough. He must keep it in line with the farther one, the stake at the remotest end of the ridge, and as he keeps the two in line his course is straight. It is the final goal which determines our immediate actions and if that is high enough, and strong enough, it will attract us like a heavenly magnet from all lesser and lower things, and hold us irresistibly to our heavenly pathway.

The supreme motive of Christ's life was devotion to the will and glory of God. "Wist ye not that I must be about My Father's business?" This was the deep conviction even upon the heart of the child (Luke 2:49). "My meat is to do the will of Him that sent Me" (John 4:34). "I seek not Mine own will but the will of the Father that sent Me" (John 5:30). "I came down from heaven not to do Mine own will but the will of Him that sent Me" (John 6:38). This was the purpose of His maturer life. "I have glorified Thee on the earth. I have finished the work thou gavest Me to do." This was His joyful cry as He finished His course and handed back His commission to the Father who sent Him. Is this the supreme object of our life, and are we pressing on to it through good report and evil report, caring only for one thing to please our Master, and have His approval at the last.

II. THE PRINCIPAL OF HIS LIFE

Every life can be summed up in some controlling principle. With some it is selfishness in the various forms of avarice, ambition or pleasure. With others it is devotion to some favorite pursuit of art or literature or invention and discovery. With Jesus Christ the one principle of His life was love, and the law that He has left for us is the same simple and comprehensive law of love, including every form of duty in the one new commandment "A new commandment I give unto you that ye love one another as I have loved you" (John 13:34; 15:12). This is not the Old Testament law of love with self in the center, "Thou shalt love thy neighbor as thyself." But this is a new commandment with Christ in the center "that ye love one another as I have loved you." Love for His Father, love for His own, love for the sinful, love for His enemies, this covered the whole life of Jesus Christ and this will comprehend the length and breadth of the life of His followers. This will simplify every question, solve every problem and sweeten every duty into a delight and make our life as His was an embodiment of that beautiful ideal which the Holy Spirit has left us in the thirteenth chapter of First Corinthians. "Love suffereth long and is kind. Love envieth not. Love vaunteth not itself, is not puffed up, doth not behave itself unseemly, seeketh not her own, is not provoked, thinketh no evil, rejoiceth not in iniquity but rejoiceth in the truth, beareth all things, believeth all things, hopeth all things, endureth all things."

III. THE RULE AND STANDARD OF HIS LIFE

Every life must have a standard by which it is regulated, and so Christ's life was molded by the Holy Scriptures. "These are the words that I spake unto you while I was yet with you that all things must be fulfilled which were written in the law of Moses, and in the prophets, and in the Psalms concerning Me" (Luke 24:44). It was necessary that Christ's life should fulfill the Scriptures and He could not die upon the cross until He had first lived out every word that had been written concerning Him. It is just as necessary that our lives should fulfill the Scriptures and we have no right to let a single promise or command in this holy Book be a dead letter so far as we are concerned. God wants us while we live to prove in our own experience all things that have been written in this Book, and to bind the Bible in a new and living edition in the flesh and blood of our own lives.

IV. THE SOURCE OF HIS LIFE

Whence did He derive the strength for this supernatural and perfect example? Was it through His own inherent and essential deity? Or did He suspend during the days of His humiliation His own self-contained rights and powers, and live among us simply as a man, dependent for His support upon the same sources of strength that we enjoy? It would seem so. Listen to His own confession (John 5:9, 30; 6:57). "The Son can do nothing of Himself but what He seeth the Father do. I can of Mine own self do nothing. As I hear I judge. As the living Father hath sent Me and I live by the Father, so he that eateth Me even he shall live by Me." This seems to make it very plain that our Lord derived His daily strength from the same source as we may receive ours, by communion with God, by a life of dependence, faith and prayer, and by receiving and being ever filled with the presence and power of the Holy Spirit. Would we therefore walk even as He walked let us receive the Holy Ghost as He did at His baptism. Let us constantly depend upon Him, and be filled with His presence. Let us live a life of unceasing prayer. Let us draw our strength each moment from Him as He did from the Father. Let our life for both soul and body be sustained by the inbreathing of His so that it shall be true of us "In Him we live and move and have our being." This was the Master's life and this may be ours. What an inspiration it is for us to know that He humbled Himself to the same place of dependence to which we stand, and that He will exalt us through His grace to the same victories which He won.

V. THE ACTIVITIES OF HIS LIFE

The life of Jesus Christ was a positive one. It was not all absorbed in self-contemplation and self-culture, but it went out in thoughtful benevolence to the world around Him. His brief biography as given by Peter is one of practical and holy activity. "He went about doing good." In His short life of three and a half years He travelled on foot over every portion of Galilee, Samaria and Judea, incessantly preaching, teaching and working with arduous toil. He was constantly thronged by the multitudes so that Luke tells us "there was not time so much as to eat." Once at the close of a busy day He was so weary that He fell asleep on the little ship amid the raging storm. Leaving His busy toil for a season of rest still the multitudes pressed upon Him, and He could not be silent. After a Sabbath of incessant labor at Capernaum we find Him next morning rising a great while before day, that He might steal from His slumbers the time to pray. His life was one of ceaseless service, and even still on His ascension throne He is continually employed in ministries of active love. So He has said to us that we must copy Him. No consecrated Christian can be an idler or a drone. "As My Father hath sent Me even so send I you." We are here as missionaries, every one of us with a commission, and a trust just as definite as the men we send to heathen lands. Let us find our work, and, like Him, "whatsoever our hand findeth to do, do it with our might."

VI. SEPARATION

The true measure of a man's worth is not always the number of his friends, but sometimes the number of his foes. Every man who lives in advance of his age is sure to be misunderstood and opposed, and often persecuted and sacrificed. The Lord Himself has said "Woe unto you when all men speak well of you. Marvel not if the world hate you. If ye were of the world the world would love his own." Like Him, therefore, we must expect often to be unpopular, often to stand alone, even to be maligned, perhaps to be bitterly and falsely assailed and driven "without the camp" even of the religious world. Two things, however, let us not forget. First let us not be afraid to be unpopular, and secondly let us never be soured or embittered by it, but stand sweetly and triumphantly in the confidence of right, and our Master's approval.

VII. THE SUFFERING LIFE

No character is mature, no life has reached its coronation, until it has passed through fire. And so the supreme test of Christ's example was suffering, and in all His sufferings He has as the apostle Peter expressed it, "Left us an example that we should follow His steps" (I. Pet. 2:21). He suffered from the temptations of Satan for "He was in all points tempted like as we are, yet without sin," and in this He has called us to follow Him in suffering and victory, for "in that He hath suffered being tempted He is able also to succor them that are tempted." He suffered from the wrongs of men, and in this He has left us an example of patience, gentleness and forgiveness, for "When He was reviled, reviled not again; when He suffered He threatened not, but committed Himself to Him that judgeth righteously." Never was He more glorious than in the hour of shame. Never was He more unselfish than in the moment when His own sorrows were crushing His heart. Never was He more victorious than when He bowed His head on the bitter cross and died for sinful men. He is the crowned Sufferer of humanity, and He calls us to suffer with Him in sweetness, submission and triumphant faith and love.

VIII. THE FINER TOUCHES OF HOLY CHARACTER

The perfection of character is to be found in the finer touches of temper and quality which easily escape the careless observer. It is in these that the character of Christ stands inimitably supreme. One of the finest portraits of His spirit is given by Paul in the third chapter of Philippians as he tells us of His humility which might have grasped at His divine rights, but voluntarily surrendered them, emptied Himself and gladly stooped to the lowest place (Phil. 2:5-8). His unselfishness in dealing with the weak and the selfish is finely expressed in (Rom. 15:1,

3, 7). "For even Christ pleased not Himself, but as it is written the reproaches of them that reproached thee fell on Me." His gentleness and lowliness is finely expressed in His own words, "Learn of Me who am meek and lowly in heart." The highest element of character is self-sacrifice, and here the Master stands forever in the front of all sacrifice and heroism.

"If any man will come after Me let him deny himself, and take up his cross and follow Me. He that will be chief among you let him be the servant of all, for even the Son of Man came not to be ministered unto but to minister and to give His life a ransom for many." Here we are taught what it means to walk even as He walked. It is the surrendered life. It is the life of self-sacrifice. So the apostle has finely expressed it in (Ephesians 5:2).

"Walk in love as Christ also has loved us, and given Himself for an offering and a sacrifice unto God for a sweet smelling savor." This is love, self-sacrifice, and this is to God as sweet as the fragrance of the gardens of Paradise. There was something in the spirit of Jesus, and there ought to be something in every consecrated life, which can only be expressed by the term sweetness. It is with reference to this that the apostle says in II. Cor. 2:15, "We are unto God a sweet savor of Christ in them that believe, and in them that perish." God give to us this heavenly sweetness that breathes from the heart of our indwelling Saviour.

The refinement of Jesus Christ is one of the most striking traits of His lovely character. Untrained in the schools of human culture, He was notwithstanding as every Christian ought to be, a perfect gentleman. His thoughtful consideration of others is often manifest in the incidental circumstances of His life. For example, when Simon Peter was distressed about the tribute money at Capernaum, and was hesitating to speak to the Master about it, the Lord "prevented him," i.e., anticipated his very thought, and sent him down to the lake to catch the fish with the coin in his mouth, and then added with fine tact "That take, and pay for Me and thee," assuming the responsibility of the debt first for Himself to save Peter's sensitiveness. Still finer was His high courtesy toward the poor sinning woman whom the Pharisees had dragged before Him. Stoopinig down He evaded her glance lest she should be humiliated before them, and as though He heard them not He finally thrust a dart of holy sarcasm into their consciences which sent them swiftly like hounds from His presence and only when they were gone did He look up in that trembling woman s face, and gently say, "Neither do I condemn thee, go and sin no more." So let us reflect the gentleness and courtesy of Christ and not only by our lives, but our "Manner of love" commend our Christianity and adorn the doctrine of God our Saviour in all things.

There is one thing more in the spirit of the Master which He would have us copy, and that is the spirit of gladness. While the Lord Jesus was never hilarious or unrestrained in the expression of His joy, yet He was uniformly cheerful, bright and glad, and the heart in which He dwells should likewise be expressed in the shining face, the springing step, and the life of overflowing gladness. There is nothing more needed in a sad and sinful world than joyous Christians. There was nothing more touching in the Master's life than the fact that when His own heart was ready to break with the anticipation of the garden and the cross He was saying to them "Let not your heart be troubled. Let My joy remain in you and your joy be full." God help us to copy the gladness of Jesus, never to droop our colors in the dust, never to hang our harps upon the willows, never to lose our heavenly blessing or fail to "rejoice evermore."

IX. BUT WE MUST HASTEN TO NOTICE FINALLY SOME OF THE POSITIVE ELEMENTS OF FORCEFULNESS AND POWER IN THE LIFE OF JESUS

It is possible to be sweet and good and yet to be weak and unwise. This was not the character of Jesus. Never was gentleness more childlike, never was manhood more mighty and majestic. In every element of His character, in every action of His life we see the strongest virility and we recognize continually that the Son of man was indeed a man in every sense of the word.

Intellectually His mind was clear and masterful and there is nothing finer in the story of His life than the calm, victorious way in which He answered and drove from His presence the keen-witted lawyers and scribes who hounded Him with their questions and who were successively humiliated and silenced before the jeering crowd until until they were glad to escape from His presence, and after that no man durst ask Him any more questions. So majestic and impressive was His eloquence that the officers that were sent to arrest Him forgot all about their commission as they stood listening to His wonderful words, and went back to their angry masters to exclaim: "Never man spake like this Man." There was about Him a dignity which sometimes rose to such a height that we read on one occasion as He set His face steadfastly to go to Jerusalem, "As they beheld Him they were amazed, and as they followed they were afraid." In the darkest hour of His agony He reached such a height of holy dignity that even Pilate gazed with admiration and pointing to Him even amid all the symbols of shame and suffering, he cried: "Behold the Man." Even in His death He was a Conqueror, and in His resurrection and ascension He arose sublime above all the powers of death and hell.

In conclusion, How shall we walk like Him?

We must receive Him to walk in us for He hath said, "I will dwell in them and walk in them."

We must study His life until the story is burned into our consciousness and impressed upon our heart.

We must constantly look upon the picture and apply it to every detail of our own conduct and so "beholding as in a glass the glory of the Lord, we shall be changed into the same image from glory to glory even as by the Spirit of the Lord."

Do not be discouraged when you meet with failure in yourself. Do not be afraid to look in the glass and see your own defects in contrast with His blameless life. It will incite you to higher things. Self-judgment is the very secret of progress and higher attainment.

Finally, let us ask the Holy Spirit whose work it is to make Jesus real to us to unveil the vision and imprint the copy upon our hearts and lives, and so shall we be "changed into the same image from glory to glory even as by the Spirit of the Lord."

Chapter 6

KEPT

"For I know whom I have believed and am persuaded that He is able to keep that which I have committed unto him against that day."
(II Tim. 1:12)

"Kept by the power of God unto salvation." (I Peter 1:5)

The more precious any treasure is, the more important is it that it be guarded and kept. The figure of our first text is that of a bank deposit and literally reads, "He is able to keep my deposits against that day." When great deposits of gold are being conveyed to the vaults of some rich bank, whole squadrons of police stand guard, and the most powerful locks, bolts, bars, and walls and the most ceaseless and sleepless vigilance of watchmen and detectives are employed to guard them. Sometimes the figure is used in a military sense. The second text is of this kind and literally should be translated, "Who are garrisoned by the power of God through faith unto salvation." What vast expenditures and mighty armaments and armies are employed to garrison the great strategic points that guard the gates of nations, such as Port Arthur, Gibraltar, Quebec, and other citadels. Sometimes the figure is used of the shepherd and his flock, "He will gather Israel and keep him as a shepherd doth his flock."

But whatever figure or phrase may be employed, the one great thought that God would convey to the hearts of His tried and suffering people is, that they are safe in His keeping, and that He is able to guard that which we have committed unto Him against that day. Let us look at some of His gracious promises to keep His people.

He will keep us wherever we may go or be. Listen to the first promise of our Divine Keeper as it was addressed to Jacob in the hour of his loneliness and fear, "Behold, I am with thee and will keep thee in all places whither thou goest; for I will not leave thee until I have done all that which I have spoken to thee of." How He kept that word to Jacob! How many the various places where providence cast his lot! The land of Laban, the cities of the Shechemites, the land of Goshen,-everywhere his covenant God guarded and kept him. He was not an attractive figure, he was not deserving of any special consideration. He was the "worm Jacob," but God loved him in his infinite grace, and kept him, disciplined him, taught him, and prepared him to be the head of Israel's tribes, and the day came when he could say, "The God that fed and led me all my life long, the angel that kept me from all evil."

Some of you may be in strange places, lonely places, hard places, dangerous places; but if you have taken Jacob's God as your covenant God, you can rest without a fear in that ancient word, "Behold, I am with thee and will keep thee in all places whithersoever thou goest; for I will not leave thee until I have done that which I have spoken to thee of."

> "To me remains nor place nor time,
> My country is in every clime,
> I can be calm and free from care
> On any shore, since God is there.
>
> "Could I be cast where Thou art not,
> That were, indeed, a dreadful lot,
> But regions none remote I call,
> Secure of finding God in all."

He will keep us as the apple of His eye. "Keep me as the

apple of the eye" (Ps. 17:8). This is a beautiful figure founded upon the sensitiveness of the eyeball to the approach of any intruding cinder or particle of dust. Instinctively the eyelid closes before the object can enter. There is no time to think, for the action is intuitive and involuntary. The idea is that we are as near to God as our eyeball is to us, and as much a part of the body of Christ as if it were really the crystalline lens of His very eyes, and that He is as sensitive to the approach of anything that could harm us as you would be to the intrusion of a floating mote or grain of dust to your sensitive eye before you can even think or pray.

> "God is the refuge of His saints,
> When storms of sharp distress invade,
> Ere we can utter our complaint.
> Behold Him present with His aid."

He will keep us in His pavilion. "Thou shalt hide them in the secret of Thy presence from the pride of man: Thou shalt keep them secretly in a pavilion from the strife of tongues" (Ps. 31:20). It does not take Him long to erect that pavilion in the most solitary place and hide His children safely within its curtains. The story is told of a Scottish assembly of faithful worshippers in one of the glens of the fatherland in the clays when the cruel Claverhouse was hunting for the blood of the saints. Suddenly the cry was made from the sentinel watching on a neighboring cliff that soldiers were coming, and the little company had been discovered. Escape was impossible, and they just knelt down and prayed, claiming this precious psalm, "Thou shalt hide them in Thy pavilion." Immediately there began to gather among the hills a thick Scotch mist, and everything was enveloped as in a curtain. Their enemies were baffled, and they quietly and securely escaped through the familiar pathways of the mountains. God had hidden them securely in His pavilion.

We may not have the same bloody foe as the Scottish Covenanters, but the strife of tongues is here with sharper swords and more cruel hate. Oh, how often we find the psalmist calling out against the envenomed words of men, "What shall be given unto thee? Or what shall be done unto thee, thou false tongue? Sharp arrows of the mighty, with coals of juniper" (Ps. 120:3, 4). But He can shield us even from these and give us a blessing for every bitter blast from human calumny. "Let him curse," said David when they tried to quiet old Shimei, who was abusing the king in the hour of his sorrow; "it may be the Lord will requite me good for his cursing this day." Wherefore let them that suffer from the strife of tongues "commit themselves to Him in well doing as unto a faithful Creator."

He will keep us in perfect peace. "Thou wilt keep him in perfect peace, whose mind is stayed on Thee, because he trusteth in Thee" (Isa. 26:3). Literally this reads, "Peace, peace." It is the double peace with God and of God. It is the Old Testament original of the Apostle's still more beautiful promise in the fourth chapter of Philippians, "Be careful for nothing; but in everything by prayer and supplication with thanksgiving let your requests be made known unto God. And the peace of God, which passeth all understanding, shall keep your hearts and minds through Christ Jesus." In both verses it is the same peace which is referred to, that deep, divine rest which Christ puts into the heart where He comes to dwell. It is the peace of God, and it passeth all understanding. It is not the result of reasoning or sight; it is not because things have changed, and we can see the deliverance coming. It comes when all is dark and strange, and we have nothing but His bare word.

The Assyrian was at the gates of Jerusalem, and there seemed no possible escape when the voice of the prophet said, "Be strong and of a good courage, fear not, neither be dismayed; for they that be with you be more than they that be with him. With us is the Lord our God to help us, and to fight our battles." And then it is added, "The people rested themselves." The Assyrian was still there, and the danger was just as imminent, but there came upon them an unreasoning and supernatural confidence, for God had undertaken their defense. We know the sequel. How easy it was for Jehovah by the touch of a single angel's hand to lay those mighty hosts silent in the dust! So God's peace comes not by sight, but by faith. Its conditions are, "Thou wilt keep him in perfect peace whose mind is stayed on thee, because he trusted in thee."

Someone tells of two competing paintings of peace for which a great prize was offered. One was a beautiful and tranquil scene, a woodland valley with a gentle streamlet softly winding through grassy banks. There were warbling birds, and happy, playing children with the flocks lying down in green pastures, and earth and heaven were at rest. The other, and the picture that won the prize, was a raging sea, flinging high its billows and its foam around a naked rock, with a ship in the distance, driving before the hurricane with every sail furled, and the seabirds whirling through the leaden clouds in wild confusion-anything but peace. But far up in a cleft of that naked rock, above the surf and sheltered from the storm, there was a dove's nest with the mother quietly spreading her soft wings above her young in perfect peace.

> When is the time to trust?
> Is it when all is calm?
> When waves the victor's palm
> And life is one great psalm
> Of peace and rest?
>
> No! But the time to trust
> Is when the waves beat high,
> And storm clouds sweep the sky,
> And faith can only cry,
> Lord help and save.

The beautiful figure of the text in Philippians is that of a garrison, the peace of God which garrisons the heart and mind.

The need of the garrison here is not because of outside, but inside foes. Nothing can harm us from the outside if we are kept in God's perfect peace. Notice also that there are two sections of this citadel that have to be garrisoned and guarded. One is the heart, the seat of doubts, and fears, and cares. The other is the mind where our thoughts become the sources of unrest, and we wonder, and worry, and look forward and back, and look everywhere, but to God. The peace of God can quiet all our thinking and hold us in stillness and sweetly say to us,

> Cease your thinking, troubled Christian,
> What avail your anxious cares?
> God is ever thinking for you;
> Jesus ev'ry burden bears.
>
> Casting all your care upon Him,
> Sink into His blessed will
> While He folds you to His bosom,
> Sweetly whisp'ring, "Peace, be still."

He will keep us by His power. This is the meaning of our second text, "Garrisoned by the power of God through faith unto salvation." It is a very fine passage. The apostle has just told us that the inheritance is kept for us up yonder. Now he tells us we are kept for the inheritance. The inheritance is reserved for you, and you are preserved for the inheritance. But while the figure of the garrison is the same as in Philippians, yet it is a different garrison. There it was peace, now it is power. The garrison of peace is to preserve the city from internal foes; the garrison of power is to protect it from its outward enemies. The one garrison polices the streets; the other mans the walls. And it adds to the force of the figure to note that the word power here in the Greek is dynamite. The garrison is armed with heavenly artillery. When first the English troops under Lord Kitchener met the vast armies of the Mahdi, the conquering leader of the fanatical hordes of the Soudan, who outnumbered them ten to one, they protected their camp by modern artillery while the Africans came against them with the old-fashioned muskets and rifles. A hundred thousand strong, that vast array hurled itself upon the little company of English soldiers and marched to the assault with flying banners, galloping horses, and splendid enthusiasm.

The historian graphically tells how quietly and confidently the English waited the onset, for they knew that they had power in their midst before which those legions could not for a moment stand. Suddenly the Maxim guns began their terrific rattle and like a hailstorm from the heavens a rain of bullets and shells was poured upon that black host, and they melted like snow before a summer sun. It was dynamite against mere human courage. God has garrisoned us with heavenly dynamite, the power of the Holy Ghost, and, like the English soldiers, we must have confidence in it, for we are kept by the dynamite of God through faith. We must count upon His mighty strength and ever go forth with the battle cry, "Thanks be unto God that always leadeth us in triumph."

He is able to keep us in the world and from the evil. This was the Master's prayer for His disciples. In John 17:15, we read, "I pray not that thou shouldest take them out of the world, but that thou shouldest keep them from the evil." Here is a double keeping. Kept from death and sickness and anything that could take us out of the world, and yet kept from the evil of the world and especially the evil one. This is a portentous phrase in the original, *tou ponero*, the Evil One. This is no abstract evil, but a great personal Devil, the adversary "who walketh about like a roaring lion, seeking whom he may devour." But the Lord's power and the Lord's keeping stand between us and his devouring jaws. He is a conquered foe, and we are to treat him as such and to go forth against him with the prestige of a victor in the name of his Conqueror, the Lord Jesus Christ. Sometimes he assails us by his wiles and sometimes by his fiery darts, but with the shield of faith we shall be able to stand against and quench them both. We must not be too frightened of the devil.

Some people get so afraid of him that they almost fear to let the Lord have right away in His own meetings. The dread of fanaticism, it is to be feared, has kept a good many well meaning people from the baptism of the Holy Spirit. Let us boldly come and take all God has for us and trust Him to keep the counterfeit away, for if we ask bread, He is not going to give us a stone, and if we ask fish and really want what He wants, He will not let us have a serpent. In the name of Jesus and through His precious blood, we shall be safe and kept from the evil one.

He is able to keep us from stumbling. Jude says, "Now unto him that is able to keep us from falling, and to present you faultless before the presence of His glory with exceeding joy." The English translation is inadequate. The word falling means stumbling. Of course, He is able to keep us from being lost, and too many Christians are content to just get through, if it be by the skin of their teeth. That is a poor, ignoble ambition. He is able to keep you even from stumbling and to present you faultless before the presence of His glory with exceeding joy. If He is able to keep you for one second, He can keep you for thirty-three million seconds, which means one whole year, and as much longer as you keep trusting Him moment by moment. Will you rise to a higher ambition and take Him to keep you even from slipping, and tripping, and stumbling?

He is able to keep you from the touch of the adversary. There is a fine promise in the last chapter of I. John. "He that was begotten of God keepeth him, and that wicked one toucheth him not." This is a different reading from the ordinary version, but it is very blessed to say, the only begotten Son keepeth the saint that trusts Him and so keepeth him that that wicked one toucheth him not. It is the old familiar picture of the fly on one side of the window and the bird on the other. The bird dashes for its prey and thinks it has it. The fly shudders and thinks so too, but there is a dash, and a thud, and some flustered feathers, and a badly frightened bird, but the fly is still there, wondering how it all did not happen. But to you and me the secret is all plain, there was something between which the bird did not see and the fly forgot. Thank God, when the devil makes his fiercest dives, there is something between. He has to get through Jesus Christ to get you; and if you only abide in simple confidence, the devil will get a good deal more hurt than you.

He is able to keep His servants and ministers. Listen. "I the Lord have called thee in righteousness, and will hold thine hand, and will keep thee, and give thee for a covenant of the people, for a light of the Gentiles "(Isa. 62:6). This blessed promise belongs primarily to the Lord Jesus, but secondarily to every other true servant of Jehovah who is abiding in Him and working for Him. God holds His ministers in His right hand and says, "Touch not mine anointed and do my prophets no harm." He is a very reckless man that lightly speaks or acts against any true servant of the Lord. Be careful how you criticize the Master's servants.

Listen. "Who art thou that judgest another man's servant? To his own master he standeth or falleth, for God is able to make him stand." "Who art thou that judgest another?" If you are serving Christ with a true heart, my brother, be not afraid. He whom the Father beholds will hold thy right hand, and keep thee, and say to thee, "Fear not, I will give men for thee and people for thy life." "I will work and who shall let it?" God will keep thee and say to thee, "I have covered thee in the shadow of Mine hand that thou mayest plant the heavens, and lay the foundations of the earth and say to Zion, Thou art my people." A single soldier of the cross standing for Jesus and trusting in Him is mightier than legions of powerful foes. Trust Him though dangers and foes surround thee and friends may often be few, the heavens will fall and earth be dissolved before He can fail one of His trusting servants.

He will keep His cause, His Church, His vineyard. "Sing ye unto her, A vineyard of red wine. I the Lord do keep it; I will water it every moment; lest any hurt it, I will keep it night and day." Isa. 27:2-3. We sometimes seem to get the idea that we are the keepers of God's cause, and that he has forgotten all about it, and we have to shout and cry to get Him to help us look after His own property. Why, dear friends, the Lord is looking after you and the cause too. "I, the Lord, do keep it, lest any hurt it, I will keep it night and day." No doubt there are dangers, trials, adversaries, but there is one thing more, the Lord. And two little words are stronger than all the D's in the dictionary, whether they be difficulty, discouragement, division, declension, the devil, or the D.Ds.- and these two words are BUT GOD.

There is a fine prophetic picture in the opening of Zechariah which was written to comfort people in troublous times. First the prophet saw four horns, coming from all directions, sharp, cruel, powerful horns, pushing and piercing everything before them. If he looked north, there was a horn there, and south, there was another there, and they were soon to meet and he would find himself between the two. If he looked east, there was a horn there, and west, there was another there, and they were meeting in his unprotected breast. Then the scene changed, and he looked and saw four carpenters coming in the same direction, and each of them had a lot of tools-a good stout ax, and a sharp saw, and no doubt a heavy maul- and soon could be heard the sound of blows of axes and the buzzing of saws, and lo, the horns had lost their points and were pounded to a jelly and were soft cushions that could not hurt anything. Beloved, God has a carpenter for every horn and if the work you are doing is His work, the gates of hell cannot prevail against it.

He is able to keep everything that is committed to Him. "I know whom I have believed, and am persuaded that he is able to keep that which I have committed unto him against that day" (II. Tim. 1:12). The great question for you and me is, how much have we really committed?

The Gospel of Healing

Chapter 1

THE SCRIPTURAL FOUNDATION

Man has a two-fold nature. He is both a material and a spiritual being. And both natures have been equally affected by the fall. His body is exposed to disease; his soul is corrupted by sin. We would therefore expect that any complete scheme of redemption would include both natures, and provide for the restoration of his physical as well as the renovation of his spiritual life. Nor are we disappointed. The Redeemer appears among men with both hands stretched out to our misery and need. In the one He holds salvation; in the other, healing. He offers Himself to us as a complete Savior; His indwelling Spirit the life of our spirit; His resurrection body the life of our mortal flesh. He begins His ministry by healing all that had need of healing. He closes it by making on the Cross a full atonement for our sin; and then on the other side of the open tomb He passes into Heaven, leaving the double commission for "all the world," and "all the days even unto the end of. the world;"--"Go ye into all the world and preach the Gospel to every creature. He that believeth and is baptized shall be saved. He that believeth not shall be damned. And these signs shall follow them that believe. In My name they shall cast out devils . . . . they shall lay hands upon the sick and they shall recover."

This was "the faith once delivered unto the saints." What has become of it? Why is it not still universally taught and realized? Did it disappear with the Apostolic age? Was it withdrawn when Peter, Paul, and John were removed? By no means. It remained in the Church for centuries and only disappeared gradually in the growing worldliness, corruption, formalism and unbelief of the early Christian centuries. With a reviving faith, with a deepening spiritual life, with a more marked and Scriptural recognition of the Holy Spirit and the Living Christ, and with the nearer approach of the returning Master Himself, this blessed Gospel of physical redemption is beginning to be restored to its ancient place, and the Church is slowly learning to reclaim what she never should have lost. But along with this there is also manifested such a spirit of conservative unbelief and cold, traditional, theological rationalism as to make it necessary that we should "contend earnestly for the faith once delivered unto the saints." First of all we must be sure of our Scriptural foundations. Faith must ever rest on the Divine Word; and the most important element in the "prayer of faith" is a full and firm persuasion that the healing of disease by simple faith in God is, beyond question, a part of the Gospel and a doctrine of the Scriptures.

The earliest promise of healing is in Exodus 15:25, 26: "There He made for them a statute and ordinance, and there he proved them, and said, If thou wilt diligently hearken to the voice of the Lord thy God, and wilt do that which is right in His sight and wilt give ear to His commandments, and keep all His statutes, I will put none of these diseases upon thee, which I have brought upon the Egyptians: for I am the Lord thy God which healeth thee." The place of this promise is most marked. It is at the very outset of their journey, like Christ's healing of disease at the opening of His ministry. It comes immediately after the passage of the Red Sea. And we know that this event was distinctly typical of our redemption, and their journey of our pilgrimage. "These things happened unto them for ensamples, and are written for our admonition, on whom the ends of the world are come." 1 Cor. 10:11. This promise, therefore, becomes ours, as the redeemed people of God. And God meets us at the very threshold of our pilgrimage with the covenant of healing, declaring that as we walk in holy and loving obedience we shall be kept from sickness, which belongs to the old life of bondage we have left behind us forever. Sickness belongs to the Egyptians, not to the people of God. And only as we return spiritually to Egypt do we return to its maladies and perils. Nay, this is not only a promise, it is "a statute and an ordinance." And so the Lord Jesus has left for us a distinct ordinance of healing in His name as sacred and binding as any of the ordinances of the Gospel.

Ps. 105:37: "He brought them forth also with silver and gold, and there was not one feeble person among their tribes." This shows us the actual fulfillment of that promise. Although they did not fulfill their part in the covenant, yet God kept His Word. And so, although our faith and obedience are often defective, yet, if Christ is our surety, and if our faith will claim His merits and His name, we too shall see the promise fulfilled.

Job 1-2: The story of Job is one of the oldest records of history. It gives us an unmistakable view of the source from which sickness comes--Satan; and the course which brings healing, taking the place of humble self-judgment of the mercy-seat. If ever a sick chamber was unveiled it was that of Uz. But we see no physician there, no human remedy, but only a looking unto God as his Avenger. And when he renounces his self-righteousness and self-vindication and takes the place where God is seeking to bring him--that of self-renunciation and humility--he is healed.

Ps. 103: 2, 3: "Bless the Lord, oh my soul, and forget not all His benefits: who forgiveth all thine iniquities, who healeth all thy diseases." The Psalms of David are a continual record of affliction. But God is always the deliverer, and God alone.

We see no human hand. As directly does he look to Heaven for the healing as he does for the pardon, and in the same breath, he cries, "Who forgiveth all thine iniquities, who healeth all thy diseases." And it is a complete healing, ALL his diseases, as universal and lasting as the forgiveness of his sins. And how glorious and entire that was, is evident enough. "As far as the East is from the West, so far hath He removed our transgressions from us." But here, as in the case of Job, there is an intimate connection between the sickness and the sin; and both must be healed together.

2 Chron. 14: 12, 13: "And Asa, in the thirty and ninth year of his reign, was diseased in his feet, until his disease was exceeding great: yet in his disease he sought not to the Lord, but to the physicians. And Asa slept with his fathers." Here was a king who had begun his reign by an act of simple implicit trust in God, when human resources utterly failed him; and by that trust (verses 9-12) he won one of the most glorious victories of history. But success corrupted him, and taught him to value too highly the arm of flesh. So that in his next great crisis (2 Chron. 16:7, 8) he formed an alliance with Syria, and lost the help of God. He refuses to take warning from the prophet, and rushes on to the climax of his earthly confidence. He becomes sick. Here is a greater foe than the Ethiopians, but again he turns to man. "He sought not to the Lord, but to the physicians." And the vivid picture of the outcome could not be more sad or sarcastic: "And Asa slept with his fathers."

Isaiah 53:4, 5. "Surely He hath borne our griefs, and carried our sorrows . . . and with His stripes we are healed."

This the great Evangelical vision, the Gospel in the Old Testament, the very mirror of the coming Redeemer. And here in the front of it, prefaced by a great AMEN--the only "surely" in the chapter is the promise of healing; the very strongest possible statement of complete redemption from pain and sickness by his life and death, and the very words which the Evangelist afterwards quotes, under the inspired guidance of the Holy

Ghost (Matt. 8:17) as the explanation of His universal works of healing. The translation in our English version does very imperfect justice to the force of the original. The translation in Matthew 8:17 is much better: "Himself took our infirmities, and bare our sicknesses." The literal translation would be, "surely He hath borne away our sicknesses and carried away our pains."

Any person who will refer to such a familiar commentary as that of Albert Barnes on Isaiah, or any other Hebrew authority, will see that the two words here used denote respectively "'sickness" and "pain," and that the words for "bear" and "carry," denote not mere sympathy, but an actual substitution and the removal utterly of the thing borne. Therefore, in the same full sense as He has borne our sins, Jesus Christ has SURELY BORNE AWAY and CARRIED OFF our sicknesses; yes, and even our PAINS, so that abiding in Him, we may be fully delivered from both sickness and pain. Thus "by His stripes we are healed." Blessed and glorious Gospel! Blessed and glorious Burden Bearer.

Thus the ancient prophet beholds in vision the Redeemer coming first as a Great Physician, and then hanging on the Cross as a Great Sacrifice. And thus the Evangelists have also described him; for three years the Great Healer, and then for six hours of shame and agony, the Dying Lamb.

Matthew 8:17. "He healed all that were sick, that it might be fulfilled which was spoken by Esaias the prophet saying, Himself took our infirmities and bare our sicknesses." This is quoted as the reason why He healed all that were sick. It was not that He might give his enemies a vindication of His Divinity, but that He might fulfill the character presented of Him in ancient prophecy. Had he not done so, He would not have been true to His own character, and if He did not still do so, He would not be--"Jesus Christ, the same yesterday, today, and forever." These healings were not occasional, but continual; not exceptional, but universal. He never turned any away. "He healed all that were sick." "As many as touched Him were made perfectly whole." He is still the same.

Now, this was the work of His life. We have been too ready to sum up all the Redeemer's work in the one act at the close; and in our zeal for the value of His blood, we have forgotten the preciousness of His earthly life. But God would not have us forget that He spent more than three years in deeds of power and love before He went up to that Cross to die. And we need that Living Christ quite as much as Christ Crucified. The Levitical types included the meat offering quite as much as the sin offering; and suffering human hearts need to feed upon the Great Loving Heart of Galilee and Bethany, as much as on the Lamb of Calvary.

It would take entirely too long to examine in detail the countless records of His healing power and grace, or tell how He cured the leper, the lame, the blind, the palsied, the impotent, the fever stricken, "all that had need of healing;" how He linked sickness so often with sin, and forgave before he spake the restoring word; how He required their own personal touch of appropriating faith, and bade them take the healing by rising up and carrying their bed; how His healing went far beyond His own immediate presence, and reached and saved the centurion's servant and the nobleman' s son; and how sharply He reproved the least question of His willingness to help, and threw the responsibility of man's suffering on his own unbelief. These and many more such lessons crowd every page of the Master's life, and still reveal to us the secret of claiming His healing power. And what right anyone can claim to explain away these miracles, as mere types of spiritual healing and blessing, and not as specimens of what He still is ready to do for all who trust Him, is as inexplicable as the Mythical Theory. Such was Jesus of Nazareth. But was this blessed power to die with Him?

John 16:12: "Verily, verily, I say unto you, He that believeth on Me, the works that I do shall he do also; and greater works shall he do, because I go to my Father." Here is another "VERILY," nay a "VERILY, VERILY." Then it must be something emphatic, and something man was sure to doubt. Now, it is no use to tell us that this meant that the Church after Pentecost was to have greater spiritual power, and do greater spiritual works by the Holy Ghost than Jesus Himself did, inasmuch as the conversion of the soul is a greater work than the healing of the body; because Jesus says, "The works that I do, shall he do also," as well as the "greater works than these:" that is, he is to do the same works Christ did, and greater also. And so we know they did the same works that he did. Even during His life He sent out the twelve Apostles, and then He sent out the seventy as forerunners of the whole host of the Christian Eldership (for the seventy were just the first Elders of the Christian Age, corresponding to the seventy Elders of Moses), with full power to heal. And when He was about to leave the world, He left on record both these Commissions in the most unmistakable terms.

Mark 16:15-18: "Go ye into all the world and preach the Gospel to every creature. He that believeth and is baptized shall be saved; he that believeth not shall be damned. And these signs shall follow them that believe: In My name they shall cast out devils, they shall speak with new tongues, they shall take up serpents, and if they drink any deadly thing it shall not hurt them, they shall lay hands on the sick and they shall recover." Here is the Commission given to them, the twofold Gospel, and assuring them of His presence and unchanging power.

What right have we to preach the one without the other? What right have we to hold back any part from the perishing world? What right have we to go to the unbelieving world and demand their acceptance of our message without these signs following? What right have we to explain their absence from our ministry by trying to eliminate them from God's Word, or consign them to an obsolete past? Nay, Christ did give them, and they did follow as long as Christians continued to "believe" and expect them. And by such "mighty signs and wonders" the Church was established in Jerusalem, Samaria, and unto the uttermost parts of the earth.

The unbelief of the world needs them today as much as in the Apostolic times. During the Apostolic age these manifestations of healing power were by no means confined to the Apostles. Philip and Stephen were as gloriously used as Peter and John. In 1 Cor. 12:9-30, "the gifts of healing" are spoken of as widely diffused and universally understood among the endowments of the Church. But now, the Apostolic age is closing; is this to be continued, and if so, by whom?

By what limitation is it to be preserved from fanaticism and presumption? By what commission is it to be perpetuated to the end of time, and placed within the reach of all God's suffering saints? We turn with deep interest to James 5:14. "Is any sick among you? let him call for the elders of the Church; and let them pray over him, anointing him with oil in the name of the Lord. And the prayer of faith shall save the sick, and the Lord shall raise him up; and if he have committed sins, they shall be forgiven him."

Now, let us notice first who gives this commission. It is James, the President of the Apostolic Board; the presiding officer of the Mother Church at Jerusalem; the one who had authority to say, in summing up the decrees of the Council at Jerusalem (Acts 15:19), "My sentence is;" the man who is named first by Paul himself among the Pillars of the Church (Gal. 2:9); he it is who rightly transmits the Apostolic gifts to the ordinary and permanent officers who are to succeed them in the oversight of the flock of Christ.

Again, observe to whom this power is committed. Not the Apostles, who are now passing away, not men and women of rare gifts and difficult of access, but the elders, the ordinary officers of every single church, the men who are within reach of every sufferer, the men who are to continue till the end of the age.

Again, notice the time at which this commission is given. Not at the beginning, but at the close of the Apostolic age; nor for that generation, but for the one that was just rising, and all the succeeding ages. For, indeed, these New Testament epistles were not widely circulated in their own age, but were mainly designed "for our admonition on whom the ends of the world are come."

Again, observe the nature of the ordinance enjoined--the prayer of faith, and the anointing with oil in the name of the Lord. Now, this was manifestly not a medical anointing, for it was not to be applied by a physician, but by an elder, and must, naturally, be the same anointing of which we read, Mark 6:13, and elsewhere, in connection with the healing of disease by the Apostles themselves. Any other interpretation would be strained and contrary to the obvious meaning of the custom, as our Lord and His Apostles observed it. In the absence of any explanation here to the contrary, we are bound to believe that it was the same--a symbolical religious ordinance expressive of the power of the Holy Ghost, whose peculiar emblem is oil. The Greek Church still retains the ordinance. The Romish apostasy has changed it into a mournful preparation for death. It is a beautiful symbol of the Divine Spirit of life taking possession of the human body, and breathing into it His vital energy.

Again, observe that this is a command. It ceases to be a mere privilege. It is the Divine prescription for disease; and no obedient Christian can safely dispense with it. Any other method of dealing with sickness is unauthorized. This is God's plan. This makes faith so simple and easy. We have but to obey in childlike confidence; He will fulfill.

And once more, we must not overlook the connection of sickness with sin, the suggestion that the trial has been a Divine chastening, and requires self-judgment, penitence and pardon, and the blessed assurance that both pardon and healing may be claimed together in His name.

3 John 2: "Beloved, I wish (pray) above all things that thou mayest prosper and be in health, even as thy soul prospereth." If more were needed than the testimony of James, the last of the Apostles, and the one who best knew the Master's heart, has left this tender prayer, by which we may know our Father's gentle care for our health as well as for our souls. And when God breathes such a prayer for us, we need not fear to claim it for ourselves. But, as we do, we must not forget that our health will be even as our soul prospers.

Eph. 5:30: "We are members of His body, His flesh, and His bones." These words recognize a union between our body and the risen body of the Lord Jesus Christ, which gives us the right to claim for our mortal frame all the vital energy of His perfect life. His body is ours. His life is ours, and it is all sufficient.

Rom.8:11. "If the Spirit of Him that raised up Jesus from the dead dwell in you, He that raised up Christ from the dead shall also quicken your mortal body by His Spirit that dwelleth in you." This cannot refer to the future resurrection. That will be by the "Voice of the Son of God," not the Holy Spirit. This is a present dwelling and a quickening by the Spirit. And it is a quickening of the "mortal body," not the soul. What can this be but physical restoration, which is the direct work of the Holy Ghost, and which only they can receive who know the indwelling of the Divine Spirit? It was the Spirit of God that wrought all the miracles of Jesus Christ on earth. Matt.7:28. And if we have the same Spirit dwelling in us we shall experience the same works.

2 Cor. 4:10, 11: "Always bearing about in the body the dying of the Lord Jesus, that the life also of Jesus might be manifested in our mortal flesh. For we which live are always delivered unto death for Jesus' sake, that the life also of Jesus might be made manifest in our mortal body. "This is Paul's physical experience, constant peril, infirmity, and physical suffering, probably by persecution and even violence; in order that the

healing, restoring and sustaining power, and life of Jesus might be the more constantly manifest in his very body for the encouragement of suffering saints, "for your sakes." His life was a constant miracle; that it might be to all men a pledge and monument of the promise made to him, for all who might hereafter suffer. "My grace is sufficient for thee." This life, he tells us, v. 16, "was renewed day by day." The healing power of Christ is dependent on our continual abiding in Him, and, like all his gifts, is renewed day by day.

Finally, as a voice that has been speaking for eighteen centuries, let us hear the sweet words, Heb. 13:8: "Jesus Christ the same yesterday, today, and forever." And this is but an echo of that voice that spoke these parting words a generation before :"Lo, I am with you always, even unto the end of the world." He did not say I will be; that would have suggested a break; but I AM, an unchanging NOW, a presence never withdrawn, a love, a nearness, a power to heal and save as constant and as free as ever, even unto the end of the world; "JESUS CHRIST, THE SAME, YESTERDAY, TODAY, AND FOREVER."

Thus have we traced the teachings of the Holy Scriptures from Exodus to Patmos: we have seen God giving His people the ordinance of healing in the very outset of their pilgrimage; we have seen it illustrated in the ancient dispensation in the sufferings of Job, the songs of David, and the sad death of Asa; we have seen Isaiah's prophetic vision of the coming Healer; we have seen the Son of Man coming to fulfill that picture to the letter; we have heard Him tell His weeping disciples of His unchanging presence with them; we have seen Him transmit His healing power to their hands; and we have seen them hand it down to us and to the permanent officers of the Church of God, until the last ages of time. And now what more evidence can we ask? What else can we do but believe, rejoice, receive, and proclaim this great salvation to a sick and sinking world?

Chapter 2

PRACTICAL DIRECTIONS

We have already considered the Scriptural grounds of the doctrine of healing by faith in God. The practical question next arises: How can one who fully believes in the doctrine receive the blessing and appropriate the healing?

Be fully persuaded of THE WORD OF GOD in this matter.

This is the only sure foundation of rational and Scriptural faith. Your faith must rest on the great principles and promises of the Bible, or it never can stand the testing of oppositions and trials which are sure to come. You must be sure that this is part of the Gospel and the redemption of Christ that all the teachings and reasonings of the best of men could not shake you. Most of the practical failures of faith in this matter result from defective or doubtful convictions of the Divine Word.

The writer may be permitted to mention the case of a lady who had fully embraced this truth and accepted Christ as her Healer. She was immediately strengthened very much both in spirit and body, and her overflowing heart was only too glad to tell the good news to all her friends. Among others, she met her pastor and told him of her faith and blessing. To her surprise, he immediately objected to any such views, warned her against this new fanaticism, and told her that these promises on which she was resting were not for us; but only for the Apostles and the Apostolic age. She listened, questioned, yielded, and abandoned her confidence. In less than one month, when the writer saw her again, she had sunk to such depression that she scarcely knew whether she even believed the Bible or not. If those promises were for the Apostles, she argued, why might not all the other promises of the Bible also be for them only? She was invited to spend a season in examining the teaching of the Word of God. The promises of healing from Exodus to James were carefully compared and every question calmly weighed, until the truth became so manifest, and its evidence so overwhelming, that she could only say, "I know it is here, and I know it is true, if all the world should deny it." Then she knelt and asked the Lord's forgiveness for her weakness and unbelief, renewed her solemn profession of faith and consecration, and claimed anew the promise of healing and the baptism of the Holy Spirit. From that day she has been restored and blessed with all spiritual blessings; until the very pastor who caused her to stumble has been forced to own that this is the finger of God. But the starting-point of all her blessing was the moment when she fully accepted and rested in the Word of God.

Be fully assured of the WILL OF GOD TO HEAL YOU.

Most persons are ready enough to admit the power of Christ to heal. The devil himself admits this. True faith implies equal confidence in the willingness of God to answer this prayer of faith. Any doubt on this point will surely paralyze our prayer for definite healing. If there be any question of this, there can be no certainty in our expectation. A mere vague trust in the possible acceptance of our prayer is not strong enough to grapple with the forces of disease and death. The prayer for healing, "if it be His will," carries with it no claim for which Satan will quit his hold. This is a matter about which we ought to know His will before we ask, and then will and claim it because it is His will. Has He given us any means by which we may know His will? Most assuredly. If the Lord Jesus has purchased it for us in His redemption, it must be God's will for us to have it, for Christ's whole redeeming work was simply the executing of the Father's will. If Jesus has promised it to us; it must be His will that we should receive it for how can we know His will but by His word? Nay, more, if Jesus has bequeathed it to us in the New Testament, which is simply HIS LAST WILL, then it is simply one of the bequests of our Brother's will, and all questions of will should end. The Word of God is forevermore the standard of His will, and that word "has declared immutably that it is God's greatest desire and unalterable principle of action and will to render to every man according as he will believe, and especially to save all who will receive Christ by faith, and to heal all who will receive it by similar faith. No one thinks of asking for forgiveness "if the Lord will." Nor should we throw any stronger doubt on His promise of physical redemption. Both are freely offered to every trusting heart that will accept them.

A very striking case recently occurred to the writer's observation. A lady, quite prominent in Christian work, had been prayed with and anointed for healing. She returned in a few weeks saying that she was no better. She was asked if she had believed fully. "Yes," she replied, "I believed that I should be healed if it was His good pleasure, and if not, I am willing to have it otherwise." "But," was the reply, "may we not know God's pleasure in this matter from His own word, and ask with the full expectation of the blessing? Indeed, ought we to ask anything of God until we have reason to believe that it is His will? Is not His word the intimation of His will, and, after He hath so fully promised it, is it not a vexation and a mockery to imply a doubt of His willingness?" She went away, and the very next morning she claimed the promise. She told the Lord that now she not only believed that He could, but would, and did remove the trouble. In less than half an hour it had wholly and visibly disappeared--and it was an external tumor of considerable size, about which there could be no imagination or mistake.

There is much subtle unbelief often in the prayer, "Thy will be done." That blessed petition really expresses the highest measure of Divine love and blessing. No kinder thing can come to us than that will. And yet we often ask it as if it was the iron hand of a cruel despot, and an inexorable destiny.

Be careful that you are yourself RIGHT WITH GOD.

If your sickness has come to you on account of any sinful cause, be sure that you thoroughly repent of and confess your sins, and make full restitution as far as in your power. If it has been a discipline designed to separate you from some evil, at once present yourself to God in frank self-judgment and consecration, and claim from Him the grace to sanctify you and keep you holy. An impure heart is a constant fountain of disease. A sanctified spirit is in itself as wholesome as it is holy. At the same time do not let Satan paralyze your faith by throwing you back on your unworthiness, and telling you that you are not good enough to claim this.

We never can deserve any of God's mercies. The only plea is the name, merits, and righteousness of Christ. But we can renounce known sin, we can walk so as to please God. We can judge in ourselves, and put away all that God shows us as wrong. The moment we do this we are forgiven. "If we would judge ourselves, we should not be judged." "If we confess our sins; He is faithful and just to forgive us our sins, and to cleanse us from all unrighteousness." Do not wait to feel forgiveness or joy, but let your will be wholly turned to God, and believe at once that you are accepted, and then draw near with a true heart in full assurance of faith, having your heart sprinkled from an evil conscience, and your body washed with pure water.

It is quite vain for us to try to exercise faith for ourselves or others in the face of willful transgression and in defiance of the chastening which God has meant we shall respect and yield to. But, when we receive His correction; and to turn to Him with humble and obedient hearts, He will graciously remove the hand of pain, and make the touch of healing the token of His forgiving love. "The prayer of faith shall save the sick, and the Lord shall raise him up; and if he have committed sins they shall be forgiven him. Confess your faults one to another, and pray one for another, that ye may be healed."

Often our sickness is but a moral malady contracted by our getting on Satan's territory. We cannot be healed until we get out of the forbidden place, and stand again on holy ground. So that this question of our personal state, while not a condition of healing, is a very important element in it. The great purpose of God in all His dealings with us is our highest welfare, and our spiritual soundness. To the suffering Christian, therefore; there is no better counsel than the old exhortation, "Let us search and try our ways, and turn again unto the Lord. He doth not afflict willingly, nor grieve the children of men. The Lord is good to those that wait for Him, to the soul that seeketh Him."

The writer would illustrate this by again referring to an actual incident: A member of his own family was suddenly attacked with violent and dangerous illness. It was a little child, so young as to make it certain that it could not be on account of any fault or sin of its own. Amid violent convulsions all human remedies were quickly dispensed with, and the case presented to God in prayer and anointing. Immediate relief was given, but the trouble was not wholly removed, and again that night a very threatening relapse occurred, and the prayer of faith seemed met by a dreadful cloud of hindrance. At once it became deeply impressed upon his heart that something was seriously wrong on the part of some member of the family. Earnest search was made, and at length it was found to be indeed so. One person had greatly sinned and covered it. But now a deep and thorough confession was made, and the wrong solemnly made right in God's sight, and His forgiveness sought and claimed. Then all the burden rolled away, and the innocent sufferer was instantly healed, and the next morning rose with the most marvelous health and buoyancy, and has not been seriously ill since.

Having become fully persuaded of the Word of God, the Will of God, and your own personal acceptance with God, NOW COMMIT YOUR BODY TO HIM AND CLAIM HIS PROMISE OF HEALING in the name of Jesus by simple faith.

Do not merely ask for it, but humbly and firmly claim it as His covenant pledge as your inheritance, as a purchased redemption right, as something already fully offered you in the Gospel, and waiting only your acceptance to make good your possession. There is a great difference between asking and claiming, between wanting and taking. You must take Christ as your Healer--not as an experiment, not as a future, perhaps, but as a present reality. You must believe that He does now, according to His promise, touch your life with His Almighty Hand, and quicken the fountains of your being with His strength. Do not merely believe that He will do so, but claim and believe that He does touch you now, and begin the work of healing in your body. And go forth counting it done and acknowledging and praising Him for it.

It is a good thing to prepare for this solemn act of committal and appropriating faith. It ought to be a very deliberate and final step, and in the nature of things it cannot be repeated. Like the marriage ceremony, it is the signalizing and sealing of a great transaction, and depends for its value upon the reality of the union which it seals. Before we take this step we ought to weigh every question thoroughly and then regard them as forever settled, and then step out solemnly, definitely, irrevocably on new ground, on God's promise, with the deep conviction that it is for ever. This gives great strength and rest to the heart, and closes the door against a thousand doubts and temptations. From that moment doubt should be regarded as absolutely out of the question, and even the very thought of retreating or resorting to old means inadmissible.

Of course, such a person will at once abandon all remedies and medical treatment. God has become the Physician, and He will not give His glory to another. God has healed, and all human attempts at helping would imply a doubt of the reality of the healing. The more entirely this act of faith can be a complete committal, the more power will it have. If you have any question about your faith for this, make it a special matter of preparation and prayer. Ask God to give you special faith for this act. All our graces must come from Him, and faith among the rest. We have nothing of our own, and even our very faith is but the grace of Christ Himself within us. We can exercise it, and thus far our responsibility extends; but He must impart it, and we simply put it on and wear it as from Him. And this makes the exercise of strong faith a very simple and blessed possibility.

Jesus does not say to us, Have great faith yourselves. But He does say to us, Have the faith of God. That is better. God's faith is all sufficient, and we can have and use it. We can take Christ for our faith as we took Him for our justification, for our victories over temptation, for our sanctification. We may thus sweetly rest in the assurance that our faith has not failed to meet the demands of the promise, for it has been Christ's own faith. We simply come in His name, and present Him as our perfect offering, our plea, our faith, our advocate, our righteousness, and our all; and we simply and utterly receive for Christ's sake our very faith itself, nothing but simply the taking of His free gift of grace. Thus come and claim His promise; and, having done so, believe according to His word that you have received it.

ACT YOUR FAITH

"Arise, take up thy bed, and walk." Not to show your faith, or display your courage, but because of your faith, begin to act as one that is healed. Treat Christ as if you trusted Him, by attempting in His name and strength what would be impossible in your own; and he will not fail you if you really trust Him, and continue to act your faith consistently and courageously.

But it is most important that you should be careful that you do not do this on any one else's faith or word. Do not rise from your bed or walk on your lame foot because somebody tells you to do so. That is not faith, but presumption. He will surely tell you to do so, but it must be as HIS LORD; and if you are walking with Him and trusting Him you shall know His voice. Your prayer, like Peter's must be, "Lord, bid me come unto Thee on the water" and He will surely bid you, if He is to heal you; but in this great and solemn work, each of us must know and see the Lord for himself.

And then, when you do go forth to act your faith, be careful not to begin to watch the result or look at the symptoms, or see if you stand. You must ignore all symptoms, and see only Him there before you, Almighty to sustain you and save you from falling. The man who digs up his seed to see if it is growing will very soon kill it at the root. The true farmer trusts nature and lets it grow in silence. So let us trust God, willing even to see the answer buried like that seed, and dying in the dark soil of discouragement, knowing that "if it die it bringeth forth much fruit."

BE PREPARED FOR TRIALS OF FAITH

Do not look always for the immediate removal of the symptoms. Do not think of them. Simply ignore them and press forward, claiming the reality, at the back of and below all symptoms. Remember the health you have claimed is not your own natural strength, but the life of Jesus manifested in your mortal flesh, and therefore the old natural life may still be encompassed with many infirmities, but at the back of it, beside it, and over against it, is the all-sufficient life of Christ to sustain your body. "Ye are dead, and your life is hid with Christ in God." But "Christ is your life;" and the life you now live in the flesh you live by the faith of the Son of God, who loved you and gave Himself for you. Do not, then, wonder if nature still will often fail you. His healing is not nature, it is grace, it is Christ, it is the bodily life of the risen Lord. It is the vital energy of the body that went up to the right hand of God; and it never faints and it never fails those who trust it.

IT IS CHRIST WHO IS YOUR LIFE; Christ's body for your body as His Spirit was for your spirit. Therefore do not wonder if there should be trials. They come to show your need of Christ and throw you back upon Him. And to know this, and so to put on His strength in our weakness, and live in it moment by moment, is perfect healing. Then, again, trials always test and strengthen faith in proportion as it is real; it must be shown to be genuine, so that God can vindicate His reward of it before the whole universe. It is thus that God increases our faith by laying larger demands upon it, and compelling us to claim and exercise more grace. "As an eagle stirreth up her nest" and tumbles out her young in mid-air to compel them to reach out their little pinions, and train them to fly, so God often pushes us off all our own props and confidences to compel us to reach out the arms and wings of faith. But for the sacrifice of Isaac, Abraham never could have attained, as he did, to the faith of the resurrection.

But, be the symptoms what they may, we must steadily believe that at the back of all symptoms God is working out His own great restoration. "For which cause we faint not, but though our outward man perish, yet the inward man is renewed day by day."

USE YOUR NEW STRENGTH AND HEALTH FOR GOD, and be careful to obey the will of the Master.

This Christ-given strength is a very sacred thing. It is the resurrection Life of Christ in us. And it must be spent as He Himself would spend it. It cannot be wasted on sin and selfishness; it must be given to God, "a living sacrifice." The strength will fail where it is devoted to the world, and sin will always bring bodily chastisement. We may, ordinarily, expect to be in health and prosper even as our soul prospers.

Nor is it enough for us to use it for ourselves; we must testify of it to others. We must tell it to the world. We must be fearless and faithful witnesses to the Gospel of full redemption. Often the testimony will have to be given under the most trying circumstances to persons who will most proudly scorn it. But the Master commands, and the church needs, that the whole counsel of God shall be declared.

And the world needs this Gospel of healing. The pagan nations need it as an evidence of Christianity. Infidelity needs it as an answer to its materialism. The great work of Foreign Missions needs it as an introduction to the Gospel among the heathen. The next great missionary movement will and must incorporate this mighty truth. And this truth will be to the work of spreading the Gospel infinitely more than the work of medical missions has been in the past.

This is not a faith that we can hold for ourselves. It is a great and solemn trust, and we who have received it must unite to use it for the glory of God, for a witness to the truth and for the spread of the Gospel, as the tongues of Pentecost were used in the ancient days of Christianity. These wonderful manifestations of the power of God which we are beginning to see, are significant signals of the end. They are the forerunners of the Great Appearing. As they marked the period of his presence on earth so they attend His return. And, they bid us prepare in solemn earnest for his Advent.

With our eyes no longer on the grave, but on the opening heavens, and our hearts feeling already some of the pulses of that resurrection life, it is ours to watch and work as none others can; not sparing ourselves in anxious self-care, but working in His great might, in season and out of season, and finding it true that "He that saveth his life shall lose it, and he that loseth his life for Christ's sake and the Gospel's shall keep it unto life eternal."

Thus let us claim, and keep and consecrate this great gift of the Gospel and the grace of God. And now "The very God of peace sanctify you wholly; and I pray God your whole spirit and soul and body be preserved blameless unto the coming of our Lord Jesus Christ. Faithful is He that calleth you, who also will do it."

Chapter 3

POPULAR OBJECTIONS

We will now refer to some of the most forcible objections to the glad tidings that "He that forgiveth all our iniquities," as truly and as fully also "healeth all our diseases."

THE AGE OF MIRACLES IS PAST: This is commonly assumed as an axiom, and almost quoted as a Bible text. In reply, let us ask, what age are we in?

There have been, and shall be, various Ages and Dispensations, viz, Paradisiacal, Antediluvian, Patriarchal, Mosaic, Christian, Millennial, Eternal. We are not in the Patriarchal or Mosaic, we are not in the Millennial, we must therefore be in the Christian. But perhaps there are two or three Christian Ages; one for Christ and His Apostles, and one for us. And yet Paul says he lived in "these last days." He speaks of the people of his generation as those on whom "the ends of the world are come." And Peter, in his sermon on the Day of Pentecost, claims for his day a prophesy of Joel for the latter days. We must then be in the Age of Christ and Christianity, and if that was not the Age of Miracles then what is it?

But perhaps there was to be a great gulf between the first and last periods of this Age. Perhaps it was only to begin with special manifestations of Divine Power and then shade down into sober commonplace. Why then should Joel say that the signal outpouring of the Holy Spirit should be "in the latter days," and the special gifts of the Spirit to the handmaids and servants, and the preternatural signs and wonders both in Earth and Heaven should be specially "before the coming of that great and terrible day of the Lord," that is, toward the close of the Christian Age, and prior to the Advent? Why also should Paul so strongly insist, in 1 Cor. 12, that the Church of Christ is one body, not two, and that the gifts of every part belong to the whole? If there be an essential difference between the Apostolic and later Age, then the Church is not one body but two; then the gifts of those members do not flow into our members; then the glorious figure and powerful reasoning of that chapter are false and delusive. If we are the same body, we have the same life and power.

What made the Apostles more mighty than ordinary men? It was not their companionship with Jesus; it was the gift of the Holy Ghost. Have we not the same? And do we not exalt the men and disparage the Spirit that makes them what they were when we speak of their power as exceptional and transient? Peculiar and exceptional functions they indeed had, as the witnesses of Christ's resurrection, and the organizers of the Church on earth; but to show to men that the miraculous gifts of the Church were not confined to them, these are specially distinguished from the Apostleship in 1 Cor. 12. They were conferred in preeminent degree on Stephen, Philip, and others who were not apostles at all, and they were committed by James to the ordinary and permanent eldership of the Church.

Nay, the dear Master never contemplated or proposed any post-apostolic gulf of impotence and failure. Man's unbelief and sin have made it. The Church's own corruption has caused it. But He never desired it nor provided for it. Standing midway between earth and heaven, and looking down to the nineteenth century with a love as tender, and a grace as full and potential, as He exercised to the first, and speaking in the present tense, as though we were all equally near to Him who would never be separated from us, He said, "All power is Given unto Me in HEAVEN AND IN EARTH, and lo, I AM with you ALL

THE DAYS, even unto the End of the AGE" (Greek). It was to be one age, not two, and His all power was never withdrawn. He was to be a perpetual AM, and to be as near at the end as at the beginning. In fact; the work we were to do was to be but the complement of His own, nay, His Own work; for Luke says, "He began to do and to teach." He must therefore be finishing His work still. And this is just what He Himself said our work would be, "He that believeth on Me, the works that I do shall he do also (that is, they shall be Christ's work and ours, in partnership), nor shall they be aught diminished by His seeming absence; for "greater works shall he do because I go to My Father."

And, indeed, so long as the ancient Church retained in even limited measure the faith and holiness of the first days, the same works were uniformly found. In the second, third, and fourth centuries, fathers as famous as Irenaeus and Tertullian, bear testimony to the prevalence of many undoubted miracles of healing, and even the raising of the dead in the name of Jesus. And as late as the fifth century supernatural events, in the case of numerous well-known and living men and women, are attested by authorities as high as Procopius and Justinian, on evidence so strong that the sober editor of Mosheim declares that he who would doubt it must be ready to question all the facts of history.

The Age of Miracles is not past. The Word of God never indicated a hint of such a fact. On the contrary, they are to be among the signs of the last day; and the very adversary himself is to counterfeit them, and send forth at last the spirits of devils working miracles, into the kings of the earth. So that the only defense against the false miracles will be the true. We are in the Age of miracles, the Age of Christ, the Age which lies between two Advents, and underneath the eye of a ceaseless Divine Presence, the Age of Power, the Age which above all other ages of time should be intensely alive.

THE SAME RESULTS AS ARE CLAIMED FOR FAITH IN THE HEALING OF DISEASE ARE ALSO SAID TO FOLLOW THE PRACTICES OF SPIRITUALISM, ANIMAL MAGNETISM, CLAIRVOYANCE, ETC.

We will not deny that while some of the manifestations of Spiritualism are undoubted frauds, there are many that are unquestionably supernatural, and are produced by forces for which Physical Science has no explanation. It is no use to try to meet this terrific monster of SPIRITUALISM in which, as Joseph Cook says, is, perhaps, the great IF of our immediate future in England and America, with the hasty and shallow denial of the facts, of their explanation as tricks of legerdemain. They are often undoubtedly real and superhuman. They are "the spirits of devils working miracles," gathering men for Armageddon. They are the revived forces of the Egyptian magicians, the Grecian oracles, the Roman haruspices, the Indian medicine-men. They are not divine, they are less than omnipotent, but they are more than human.

Our Lord has expressly warned us of them, and told us to test them, not by their power, but by their fruits, their holiness, humility, and homage to the name of Jesus and the Word of God; and their very existence renders it the more imperative that we should be able to present against them--like the rod of Moses which swallowed the magicians, and at last silenced their limited power--the living forces of a holy Christianity in the physical as well as the spiritual world.

THE MIRACLES OF CHRIST AND HIS APOSTLES WERE DESIGNED TO ESTABLISH THE FACTS AND DOCTRINES OF CHRISTIANITY; WE DO NOT NEED THEIR CONTINUANCE.

Why, then, do the critics call in question the existence of these facts and the credibility of these writings? How are the inhabitants of new countries to know the divinity of these oracles? What access have they, or indeed the great masses of men everywhere, to the archives of learning, or the manuscripts of the Bible? Nay, every generation needs a living Christ, and every new community needs "these signs following," to confirm the word. And we have sometimes seen the plausible and persistent Agnostic, whom no reason could satisfy, silenced and confounded when brought face-to-face with some humble, illiterate woman, as she told him with glowing honesty, which he felt in the depths of his heart, that she had been raised up from lifelong helplessness by the word and name of Jesus only. Until he comes again the world will never cease to need the touch of His Power and Presence, "God also bearing them witness both with signs and wonders, and gifts of the Holy Spirit according to His own will."

There is also a current misapprehension about the full design of Christ's miracles which takes away one-half their beauty and value. They are looked upon solely and mainly as special testimonies to Christ's power and divinity. But if this had been all, a few special and marked cases would have been sufficient. He would not then have healed the thousands who daily thronged Him. But we are told, on the contrary, that they were not isolated and occasional, but numerous and almost universal. "He healed all that had need of healing, and all that were sick and, not so much as a proof of His power, as to show that which He now wished them to know--His boundless love--to fulfill the ancient prophetic picture of the blessed Christ, and that it might be fulfilled that was spoken by the prophet Esaias, "Himself took our infirmities, and bare our sicknesses."

But if it was necessary for Him to fulfill that character then, it is as much so still; as necessary yet that He should never cease to be true to the picture God drew of Him, which He drew of Himself. If this be not true still for us, then "Jesus Christ is" NOT "the Same, yesterday, today, and forever." If this be not still true for us, then, perhaps, the other promises of the Scripture are not also true for us, and He has not borne our sins any more than our sickness and suffering. Nay, "His heart is still the same:

> Kinsman, Friend and Elder Brother,
> Is His everlasting name;
> Thou art All in All to me,
> Living One of Bethany."

A common objection is urged in this way: Christ's last promise in Mark embraces much more than healing; but if you claim one, you must claim all. If you expect the healing of the sick, you must also include the gift of tongues and the power to overcome malignant poisons; and if the gift of tongues has ceased, so in the same way has the power over disease. We cheerfully accept the severe logic, we cannot afford to give up one of the promises. We admit our belief in the presence of the Healer in all the charismata of the Pentecostal Church. We see no reason why an humble servant of Christ, engaged in the Master's work, may not claim in simple faith the power to resist malaria and other poisons and malignant dangers; and we believe the gift of tongues was only withdrawn from the early Church as it was abused for vain display, or as it became unnecessary for practical use, through the rapid evangelization of the world; and it will be repeated as soon as the Church will humbly claim it for the universal diffusion of the Gospel. Indeed, instances are not wanting now of its apparent restoration in missionary labors, both in India and Africa.

Perhaps no objection is more strongly urged than the glory that redounds to God from our submission to His will in sickness, and the happy results of sanctified affliction. Well, if those who urge and claim to practice this suggestion would really accept their sickness, and lie passive under it, they would at least be consistent. But do they not send for a doctor, and do their best to get out of this sweet will of God? Is this meekly submitting to the affliction, and does not the submission usually come when the result is known to be inevitable?

We do not deny the happy results of many a case of painful sickness in turning the soul from some forbidden path and leading it into deeper experiences of God; nor do we question the deep and fervent piety, and spiritual advancement of many an invalid who cannot trust God for healing; but we are sure there is an immense amount of vague and unscriptural misunderstanding with respect to the principles of Christian discipline. We do not believe that God chastens an obedient child simply to make it good.

"FOR THIS CAUSE MANY ARE WEAK AND SICKLY AMONG YOU, AND MANY SLEEP; FOR IF WE WOULD JUDGE OURSELVES WE SHOULD NOT BE JUDGED."

Here is a definite and unchangeable law of God's dealings with His dear children. When we are judging ourselves we shall not be judged. While we hearken and obey, He "will put none of these diseases upon us which He brought upon the Egyptians." His normal state for His faithful children is soundness of body, soul and spirit (1 Thess. 5:23). His own prayer for them is that they may be in health and prosper even as their souls prospers. His will for them is to act in these things according to His word. It is ever "the good pleasure of His goodness," and "that good and perfect and acceptable will of God." "Many," it is true, "are the afflictions of the righteous;" but it is also true that "the Lord delivereth him out of them all. He keepeth all his bones: not one of them is broken."

And between "affliction" and sickness it must be well remembered there is a very clear distinction. At Marah, the children of Israel had to drink of bitter water, and it was only sweetened, not removed; as many a trial is sanctified and blessed. But it was right there that He made a statute and an ordinance of healing, and told them that if they would obey Him, they should not be sick, and He would be their constant Healer, thus showing them that Marah was not sickness. And in exact parallel, James says to us, 5:13, "is any afflicted? let him pray;" that is, for grace and strength. But, "Is any sick? let him call for the elders of the Church," and be healed. Affliction is "suffering with Christ;" and He was not sick. "In the world ye shall have tribulation;" but all the more we need a sound, strong heart, to bear and overcome.

It is objected that it is presumptuous to claim the healing of disease absolutely, and that the model of all true prayer is Christ's language in the garden: "If it be possible, let this cup pass: nevertheless not My will, but Thine be done." Yes, but they have forgotten that He knew it was not possible that this cup should pass, that in this case He was asking something which, to say the very least, He had no promise or warrant to, and which He repudiated instantly, saying, "Save me from this hour; but for this cause came I unto this hour. Father, glorify Thy Name."

Certainly, in any such circumstances, when prompted by extreme distress to ask for something for which we have no clear warrant, promise or favorable intimation of the Divine will, we ought ever to refer the matter to the arbitration of that unknown will. But when we know from His own word to us that a blessing is in accordance with His will, that it is provided for, purchased and promised, is it not really evasive, uncandid, disingenuous, and really an affectation to come to Him in doubt and uncertainty, or couching our requests in the language of ambiguity? Is it not very much the same as if a son at college should still keep writing and asking your permission for things wherein you had already written the fullest directions in your first letter? Did Christ thus pray, when He asked for things He knew to be consistent with God's will? Is it not as lawful for us to imitate Him in one prayer as another, at Bethany equally with Gethsemane? And there, what did He say? "Father, I know Thou hearest Me always," and again, "Father, I will that they be with Me." In His name may we not pray even as He, where His will is clearly made known? "If ye abide in Me, and My words abide in you, ye shall ask what YE WILL, and it shall be done unto you." Do we pray in indefiniteness when we ask for forgiveness? We take it and claim it, and being strong in faith, we thus most effectually glorify God.

WE ARE TOLD THAT THERE ARE MANY CASES OF FAILURE; and Paul and his companions are first enumerated. Paul's inevitable thorn is kept as a precious relic to torment doubting Christians; and Trophimus and Epaphroditus are dragged forward on their couches to encourage the willing patient in the hospital of Doubting Castle. With regard to Paul's thorn we must say,

FIRST: It is very uncertain if it was DISEASE; it was a messenger of Satan to BUFFET him, i.e., some humiliation--perhaps stammering.

SECONDLY: It was so far healed and more than healed, whatever it was, that it brought the power of Christ to rest upon him so mightily that he was abundantly enabled for all his labors and duties, and longed for more such provocations of blessing. And he who can see in this a feeble invalid laid aside from work, is afflicted with spiritual cross eyes.

THIRDLY: Before people can claim that their sickness is a heavenly visitation like Paul's to keep them from being exalted above measure, they would need to have been up in the third heaven with him and heard things unlawful for a man to utter! And

FOURTHLY: Paul does give us elsewhere the account of his healing (2. Cor. 1:10); and it was unmistakably by believing prayer and mighty faith even in God that raises the dead. As to Epaphroditus, he was healed through God's mercy. Trophimus, doubtless, was also, although it must have been delayed. Healing, even by faith, is not always instantaneous. There are "miracles" and "gifts of healing," the one sudden and stupendous, the other simple and probably gradual. That Trophimus should have been himself to blame for his illness or slowness of faith is not wonderful, and that there should be only two such cases in all these inspired personal sketches is most wonderful.

There are still cases of failure, but they may be accounted for, perhaps through defective knowledge or unbelief, disobedience to God in some way, failure to follow consistently the teachings of the Word and the Spirit or for a deeper spiritual discipline. And there are failures in the spiritual life--from the same or similar causes--which in no way disprove the reality of the Divine promises or the sufficiency of Christ's grace.

"LET GOD THEN BE TRUE," EVEN IF "EVERY MAN" BE "A LIAR."

But we are told, if these things be so, people should never die. Why not? Why should faith go farther than the Word? Anything beyond that is presumption. The Word places a limit to human life, and all that Scriptural faith can claim is sufficiency of health and strength for our life-work and within its fair limits. It may be longer or shorter, but it need not, like the wicked, fail to live out half its days. It should be complete, satisfying, and as long as the work of life is yet undone. And then, when the close comes, why need it be with painful and depressing sickness, as the rotten apple falls in June from disease, and with a worm at the root? Why may it not be rather as that ripe apple would drop in September, mature, mellow, and ready to fall without a struggle into the gardener's hand? So Job pictures the close of a good man's life as the full maturity of "the shock of corn that cometh in its season."

RESORT TO THE DOCTORS

We are asked by some, did not God make all these means, and does He not want us to use them? And, indeed, is it not presumption for us to expect Him to do anything unless we do all we can for ourselves? We answer, first: God has nowhere prescribed medical means, and we have no right to infer that drugs are ordinarily His means. They are not, as food, again and again referred to as necessary or enjoined for our use.

It is a most singular and unanswerable fact that in the whole history of the patriarchs no reference is made to the use of such means. In the story of Job, so full of vivid details, everybody else is described but the doctor, and everything in the universe but drugs. There is no physician in attendance, or surely we should have caught a glimpse of him in that chamber and when Job recovers, it is wholly from God's direct hand, and when he himself gets down in his true place of humility to God and love to man. In the still more elaborate prescriptions, prohibitions and enactments of the Book of Leviticus about all the details of human life, even including the disease of leprosy, there is no remote intimation of a doctor or a drug store. And it is not until after the time of Solomon, and the importation, no doubt, of Egypt's godless culture and science, that we find the first definite case of medical treatment; and there the patient dies, and dies under the stigma of unbelief and declension from God.

In the New Testament such "means" are referred to in hardly more complimentary terms, when the woman who touched the hem of His garment is described. If Luke were a physician, he abandoned his practice for evangelistic work, as may be strongly inferred from his itinerant life; for no practice could be maintained in such circumstances. Without going further, this much at least is clear:

FIRST, that God has not prescribed medicine.

SECONDLY, He has prescribed another way in the Name of Jesus, and provided for it in the atonement, appointed an ordinance to signalize it, and actually commanded and enjoined it.

And THIRDLY, all the provisions of grace are by FAITH, not by works. The use of remedies, if successful, usually gives the glory to man, and God will not do so. If the healing of sickness is one of the purchases of Christ's atonement, and one of His prerogatives as our Redeemer, then He is jealous for it, and we will also be jealous. If it be part of the scheme of salvation, then we know that the whole scheme is framed according to the "law of faith" if the language of James be a command, then it excludes the treatment of disease by human remedies as much as the employment of one physician would exclude the treatment of another at the same time and for the same case. If it be God's way of healing, then other methods must be man's ways, and there must be some risk in deliberately repudiating the former for the latter.

We do not imply by this that the medical profession is sinful, or the use of means always wrong. There may be, there always will be, innumerable cases where faith is not exercised; and if natural means have, as they do have, a limited value, there is ample room for their exercise in these. But for the trusting and obedient child of God there is the more excellent way which His Word has clearly prescribed, and by which His name will be ever glorified afresh, and our spiritual life continually renewed.

The age is one of increasing rationalism, and unbelief is constantly endeavoring to eliminate all traces of direct supernatural working from the universe, and explain everything by second causes and natural development; and God, for this very reason, wants to show his immediate working wherever our faith will afford Him an opportunity. The Higher Criticism is industriously taking the miraculous from our Bibles, and a lower standard of Christian life is busy taking all that is divine out of our life. Let all who believe in a living God be willing to prove to a scoffing generation that "the everlasting God, the Creator of the ends of the earth, fainteth not, neither is weary," for "in Him we live and move and have our being," and that still there is "nothing too hard for the Lord."

We will only refer in conclusion to the objection that these views of the truth UNDULY EXALT THE BODILY LIFE, and direct the minds of men from the transcendent interest of the immortal soul, promoting fanaticism, besides leading to other evils. The same objection might be brought against the earlier years of our Lord's ministry, when the healing of the body was made an avenue to reach men's souls, and a testimony of His spiritual teachings.

The doctrine of Christ's healing power is so closely linked with the necessity of holiness, and the deeper truths and experiences of the spiritual life, that it tends, in a preeminent degree, to promote purity and earnestness. The power which heals the body usually imparts a much richer baptism of the Holy Ghost to the heart, and the retaining of this Divine life and health requires such constant fellowship with God, and such consecrated service for the Master, that the spiritual results far outweigh the temporal; and it is one of the most powerful checks and impulses in the lives of those that have truly received it.

The abuses complained of will usually be found connected with false teaching and unscriptural perversions of those things which rash or ambitious persons disseminate for their own ungodly ends. The true doctrine of healing through the Lord Jesus Christ is most humbling, holy, and practical; it exalts no man, it spares no sin, it offers no promises to the disobedient, it gives no strength for selfish indulgence or worldly ends, but it exalts the name of Jesus, glorifies God, inspires the soul with faith and power, summons to a life of self-denial and holy service, and awakens a slumbering Church and an unbelieving world with the solemn signals of a living God and a returning Master.

Extravagances, perversions, and counterfeits, we know there are; unauthorized and self-constituted healers, mercenary impostors, who give out that they are "some great one," rash and indiscriminate anointings of persons who only bring discredit on the truth by their ignorance and inconsistency, and wolves in sheep's clothing, who claim the name of Jesus for the passes of clairvoyance, the sorcery of spiritualism, and the performances of animal magnetism. But the truth of God is not chargeable with human error, and the counterfeit is often the best testimonial to the genuine. Let the ministers of the Lord Jesus answer and set aside these evils by claiming and exercising, in the power of the Holy Ghost, the gifts and offices once delivered to them, and let the people of God, in these perilous times, "discern between the righteous and the wicked, between him that serveth God and him that serveth Him not."

Chapter 4

PRINCIPLES OF DIVINE HEALING

There are certain principles underlying all the teachings of the Holy Scriptures with respect to healing; which it is important to understand and classify and which, when rightly understood, are most helpful to intelligent faith.

THE CAUSES OF DISEASE and suffering are distinctly traced to the Fall and sinful state of man. If sickness were part of the natural constitution of things, then we might meet it wholly on natural grounds, and by natural means. But if it be part of the curse of sin, it must have its true remedy in the great Redemption. That sickness is the result of the Fall, and one of the fruits of sin no one can surely question. Death, we are told, hath passed upon all, for that all have sinned, and the greater includes the less. It is named among the curses of Deuteronomy, which God was to send for Israel's sin. Again, it is distinctly connected with Satan's personal agency. He was the direct instrument of Job's suffering, and our Lord definitely attributed the diseases of His time to his direct power. It was Satan who bound the paralyzed woman these eighteen years; and it was demoniacal influence which held and crushed the bodies and souls of those He delivered. If sickness be the result of evil spiritual agency, it is most evident that it must be met and counteracted by higher spiritual force, and not by mere natural treatment.

And again, on the supposition that sickness is a divine discipline and chastening it is still more evident that its removal must come, not through mechanical appliances, but through spiritual causes. It would be both ridiculous and vain for the arm of man to presume to wrest the chastening-rod from the Father's hand by physical force or skill. The only way to avert His stroke is to submit the spirit in penitence to His will, and seek in humility and faith His forgiveness and relief; so that from whatever side we look at disease, it becomes more and more evident that its remedy must be found alone in God and the Gospel of His Redemption.

If the disease be the result of the fall, we may expect it to be embraced in the provisions of Redemption, and would naturally look for some intimation of a remedy in THE PREPARATORY DISPENSATION which preceded the Gospel. Nor are we disappointed. The great principle that God's care and providence embraces the temporal and physical needs of his people as well as the spiritual, runs all through the Old Testament. Distinct provision for Divine healing is made in all the ordinances of Moses. And the prophetic picture of the Coming Deliverer is that of a great Physician as well as a glorious King and gracious Savior. The healing of Abimelech, Miriam, Job, Naaman and Hezekiah; the case of the Leper and the Brazen Serpent, the statute at Marah, and the blessings and curses at Ebal and Gerizim, the terrible rebuke of Asa, the one hundred and third Psalm, and the fifty-third chapter of Isaiah, leave the testimony of the Old Testament clear and distinct that the redemption of the body was the Divine prerogative and plan.

THE PERSONAL MINISTRY OF JESUS CHRIST is the next great stage in the development of these principles. His own life was a complete summary of Christianity; and from His words and works we may surely gather the great intent of redemption. And what was the testimony of His life to physical healing? He went about their cities healing all manner of sickness and disease among the people. He healed all that had need of healing, that it might be fulfilled which was spoken by Isaiah the Prophet, "Himself took our infirmities, and bare our sicknesses." Now, when we remember that this was not an occasional incident, but a chief part of His ministry; that He began His work with it, that He continued it to the close of His life; that He did it on all possible occasions and in every variety of cases, that He did it heartily, willingly, and without leaving any doubt or question of His will; that He distinctly said to the doubting leper, "I will," and was only grieved when men hesitated to fully trust Him and when we realize that in all this He was but unfolding the real purpose of His great redemption, and revealing His own unchanging character and love, and that he has distinctly assured us that He is still "the same yesterday, today, and for ever" -- surely we have a great principle to rest our faith upon, as secure as the Rock of Ages.

But redemption finds its center IN THE CROSS of Jesus Christ, and there we must look for the fundamental principle of Divine healing. It rests on the atoning sacrifice of the Lord Jesus Christ. This necessarily follows from the first principle we have stated. If sickness be the result of the Fall, it must be included in the atonement of Christ, which reaches —- "Far as the curse is found."

But, again, it is most distinctly stated in the 53rd chapter of Isaiah, as we have seen: He is said to have borne our sickness and carried our pains, the word "bear" being the very same used for the atonement of sin; the same used elsewhere to describe the act of the scapegoat in bearing away the people's guilt and the same used in the same chapter with respect to His "bearing the sins of many." In the same sense, then, as He has borne away our sins has he also borne our sicknesses. And Peter also states that "He bare our sins in His own body on the tree . . . by whose stripes we are healed." In His own body He has borne ALL OUR BODILY LIABILITIES for sin, and our bodies are set free. That one cruel "stripe" of His -- for the word is singular -- summed up in it all the aches and pains of a suffering world; and there is no longer need that we should suffer what He has sufficiently borne. Thus our healing becomes a great redemption right, which we simply claim as our purchased inheritance through the blood of His Cross.

But there is something higher even than the Cross. It is THE RESURRECTION of our Lord. There the Gospel of Healing finds the fountain of the deepest life. The death of Christ destroys the root of sickness: sin. But it is the life of Jesus which supplies the source of health and life for our redeemed bodies. The body of Christ is the living fountain of all our vital strength. He who came forth from Joseph's tomb, with the new physical life of the resurrection, is the Head of His people for life and immortality.

Not for Himself alone did He receive the power of an endless life, but as our life. He gave Him to be Head over all things for His Church, which is His body. We are members of His body, His flesh, and His bones. The healing which Christ gives us is nothing less than His own new physical life infused into our body from His own very heart, and bringing us into fellowship with His own inmost being. That Risen and Ascended One is the fountain and measure of our strength and life. We eat His flesh and drink His blood, and He dwelleth in us, and we in Him. As He lived in the Father, so he that eateth Him shall live by Him. This is the great, the vital, the most precious principle of physical healing in the name of Jesus. It is the very life of Jesus manifested in our mortal flesh.

It follows from this, that it must be wholly A NEW LIFE. The Death and Resurrection of Jesus Christ have made an awful gulf between the present and past of every redeemed life. Henceforth, if any man be in Christ, he is A NEW CREATION. Old things have passed away, ALL THINGS HAVE BECOME NEW. The death of Jesus has slain all our old self.. The life of Jesus is the spring of all new life. This is true of our physical life. It is not the restoration of the old natural strength to life. It is not the building up of our former constitution. It is the letting go of all the old dependencies. It is often the failure and decay of all our natural strength. It is a strength which "out of weakness is made strong," which has no resources to start with; which creation-like, is made out of nothing; which resurrection-like, comes out of the dark tomb, and the extinction of all previous help and hope. This principle is of immense importance in the practical experience of healing. So long as we look for it in the old natural life, we shall be disappointed. But when we cease to put confidence in the flesh, and look only to Christ and His supernatural life in us for our strength of body as well as spirit, we shall find that we can do all things through Christ that strengtheneth us.

It follows from this that the physical redemption which Christ brings, is NOT MERELY HEALING, BUT ALSO LIFE. It is not the readjustment of our life on the old basis, leaving it thenceforward to go like a machine upon the natural plane, but it is the infusion of a new kind of life and strength. Therefore it is as fully within the reach of persons in health as those who are diseased. It is simply a higher kind of life, the turning of life's water into His heavenly wine.

Therefore, it must also be kept by constantly abiding in Him, and receiving from Him. It is not a permanent deposit, but a daily dependence, a renewing of the inward man day by day, a strength which comes only as we need it, and continues only while we dwell in Him. Such a LIFE is a very sacred thing. It gives a peculiar sanctity to every look, tone, act, organ and movement of the body. We are living on the life of God, and we must live like Him and for Him. A body thus divinely quickened adds tenfold power to the soul, and all the service of the Christian life. Words spoken in this Divine energy, works done through the very life of God, will be clothed with a positive effectiveness which must make men feel that the body as well as the spirit is indeed the very Temple of the Holy Ghost.

The great agent in bringing this new life into our life is THE HOLY GHOST. The redemption work of Jesus cannot be completed without His blessed ministry. Not as a visible physical presence does this Jesus of Nazareth now meet the sick, and halt, and blind, but through a spiritual manifestation. It has all the old physical power, and produces all the ancient results upon the suffering frame, but the approach is spiritual, not physical.

The presence must be brought to our consciousness; the contact of our need with His life must come through the Holy Spirit. So Mary had to learn in the very first moment of the resurrection. "Touch me not -- I ascend." Thus, henceforth, must she know Him as the Ascended One. So Paul had ceased to know Christ Jesus after the flesh. So He had to guard the disciples at Capernaum, where, speaking of the Living Bread -- the Source of healing -- He adds: "What and if ye shall see the Son of man ascend up where He was before? It is the Spirit that quickeneth; the flesh profiteth nothing."

This is the reason why many find it hard to meet the Healer. They do not know the Holy Ghost. They do not know God spiritually. The sun in the heavens would be but a cold and glaring ball of ice were it not for the atmosphere which brings His warmth and light to us and diffuses them through our world. And Christ's life and love cannot reach us without the intermediate Spirit, the Light, the Atmosphere, the Divine Medium who brings and sheds abroad His life and light, His love and Presence in our being, the taking of the things of Jesus and showing them to us, extracting the very essence of His life and frame, and sweetly diffusing it through every vessel, nerve, organ and function of our being.

Yes, He is the great Quickener. It was through the Holy Ghost that Jesus cast out devils on earth,

and now, if the Spirit of Him that raised up Jesus from the dead dwell in you, He that raised up Christ from the dead shall also quicken your mortal body through His Spirit that dwelleth in us.

This new life must come, like all the blessings of Christ's redemption, as the FREE GRACE OF GOD, WITHOUT WORKS, AND WITHOUT DISTINCTION OF MERIT OR RESPECT OF PERSONS.

Everything that comes through Christ must come as grace. There can be no works mingled with justifying faith, except those which come after justification, and as its fruits. Any others are dead works, and fatal to our salvation. Even so, our healing must be wholly of God, or not of grace at all.

IF CHRIST HEALS HE MUST DO IT ALONE

This principle ought to settle for ever the question of using means in connection with faith for healing. The natural and the spiritual, the earthly and the heavenly, the works of man and the grace of God, cannot be mixed, any more than you could expect to harness a tortoise with a locomotive, or make a great sea cable part of iron and part of hemp. They cannot work together. The gifts of the Gospel are Sovereign gifts. God can do the most difficult things for us Himself. But HE CANNOT HELP OUR SELF-SUFFICIENCY to do the easiest. A hopeless case is therefore much more hopeful than one where we think we can do something ourselves. We must —

> "Venture on Him, venture wholly,
> Let no other trust intrude."

If healing is to be sought by natural means, let us get all the best results of skill and experience. But if it is to be through the name of Jesus it must be by GRACE ALONE.

It follows also in the same connection that if it be a part of the Gospel and a gift of Christ, it must be an impartial one, limited only by the great "whosoever" of the Gospel. It is not a special gift of discriminating favoritism, but a great and common heritage of faith and obedience. It is "Whosoever will, let him take the water of life freely." It is true all who come must conform to the simple conditions of obedient faith; but these are impartial without respect of persons, and within the reach of all.

The simple condition of this great Blessing, alike the condition of all the blessings of the Gospel is: FAITH WITHOUT SIGHT. Grace without works and faith without sight must always go together as twin principles of Glorious Gospel. The one thing God asks from all who are to receive His grace is that they shall trust His simple word where they have nothing else but His word to trust. But this must be real trust. It must believe and doubt not. If God's word be true at all it is absolutely and utterly true.

A very small grain of mustard seed will do, and it will split open with its living roots the great rocks and mountains, but it must be an entire grain. The grain must be in its integrity. One little laceration will kill its life. And one doubt will destroy the efficiency of faith; and therefore it must begin in the soul, taking God simply and nakedly at His word. A faith that is going to wait for signs and evidence will never be strong. Plants that begin by leaning will always be fragile and need a trellis. Indeed the faith which rests upon seeing is not faith. Blessed are they who have not seen, and yet have believed.

Abraham had to believe God and take the new name of faith and fatherhood before there was any indication of probability and when, indeed, every natural sign contradicted and stultified it. It is beautiful to notice the form of expression in Genesis 17. First he is told, "I will make thee a father of many nations." Then comes the change of Abraham's name which was the profession of his faith, and the acknowledgment before a scorning world that he believed God. Then follows God's next word. But how wonderful! The tense is completely changed. It is no longer a promise, but an accomplished fact; "I HAVE MADE THEE a father of many nations." It is done. Faith has turned the future into the past, and now God calls the things that are not as though they were. So we must believe, and receive the healing life of Jesus and all the blessings of the Gospel.

THE OBLIGATION

Is there any principle involving the obligation of faith in reference to physical healing? Is it an optional matter with us how we shall be healed, and whether we shall trust God or look to man? Is it "an ordinance and a statute" for us, and a matter of simple obedience? Is it His great prerogative to deal with the bodies He has redeemed, and an impertinence for man, and unsanctified man, to tamper with them, and an equal impertinence for us to choose some other way than His? Is the Gospel of salvation a commandment as well as a promise, and is the Gospel of healing of equal authority? Has He chosen to legislate about the way in which the plague which has entered His world shall be dealt with, and have we any business to interfere with His great Health Laws? HAS HE AT ENORMOUS COST, PROVIDED A REMEDY FOR HIS CHILDREN as part of His redemption, and IS HE JEALOUS FOR THE HONOR AND RIGHTS OF HIS DEAR SON'S NAME in this matter? Does He claim to be the owner of His children's bodies, and does He claim the right to care for them? Has He left us one great prescription for disease, and is any other course, unauthorized, disobedient, and at our own risk? Surely these questions answer themselves, and leave but one course open to every simple and obedient child of God.

THE ORDER of God's dealings with our souls and bodies is regulated by certain fixed principles.

A. He works from within outwards, beginning with our spiritual nature and then diffusing his life and power through our physical being. Many persons come to God for healing whose spiritual life is wholly defective and wrong. God does not refuse the healing, but He begins in the depths of the soul, and when it is prepared to receive His life, he can begin to heal the body.

B. There is a constant parallel between the state of the soul and body. John prays that Gaius "may be in health and prosper, EVEN AS his soul prospereth." A little cloud of sin upon the heart will leave a shadow upon the brain and nerves and a pressure upon the whole frame. A malicious breath of spiritual evil will poison the blood and depress the whole system. And a clear, calm and confident spirit will bring vigor into all the physical life, and open the way for all the full strong pulses of the Lord's own life in us.

C. Hence, also, healing will often be gradual in its development, as the spiritual life grows and faith takes a firmer hold of Christ. The principle of the Divine life, like the natural, is "first the blade; then the ear; after that the full corn in the ear. There must ever be much preliminary work. The seed must be planted and die." "The stalk must rise and grow strong enough to bear its heavy fruit. Many persons want the head of wheat while the blade is yet tender. Now it would only overwhelm us by its weight. We must have deep and quiet strength to sustain our higher blessing. Sometimes this preparation is all completed beforehand. Then God can work very rapidly. But in each case He knows the order and process best adapted to the development of the whole man, which is ever His great end in all His workings in us.

THE LIMITATIONS of Healing are also fixed by certain principles.

A. It is not the immortal life. Why should people ever die if Christ will always heal? Because faith can only go as far as God's promise, and God has nowhere promised that we shall never die during this Dispensation. The promise is fullness of life and health and strength up to the measure of our natural life, and until our life-work is done. True, it is the life of the resurrection which we have; but it is not the whole of it, but only the first fruits. In speaking of our immortal life in 2 Cor. 5:5, the Apostle says: "Now He that hath wrought us for this selfsame thing is God, who also hath given us the earnest of the Spirit" That is, as our earnest was a handful of the very soil of the purchased farm, but only a handful, so God has given us now, by His Spirit, in our new physical life, a handful of the very life of the resurrection. But it is only a handful, and the fullness will not come until His coming. But that handful is worth all the soil of earth and the natural life a hundredfold.

B. The next limitation has reference to the measure and degree in which we can expect this life in our present state. Shall we have strength for all sorts of supernatural exploits and extraordinary exertions? We have the promise of sufficient strength for all the will of God and all the service of Christ. But we shall have no strength for mere display, and certainly none to waste in recklessness, or spend in selfishness and sin. Within the limits of our God-appointed work, and these limits may be very wide -- much wider than any mere natural strength -- we can do all things through Christ that strengtheneth us, and may fearlessly undertake all labors, self-denials, and difficulties in the face of exposure, weakness, unhealthy conditions of climate, and the most engrossing demands upon strength and time, where Christ clearly leads and calls us; and we shall have His protecting power and find that "God is able to make all grace abound so that we, always having all sufficiency in all things, may abound unto every good work." But let us touch the forbidden earth, get out of that sacred circle of His will, or spend our strength on self or sin, and our life will wither -- like Jonah's gourd and Samson's arm. Yes, it must be true in our life; all true -- not one part wanting, "OF Him, and THROUGH Him, and TO HIM - are all things to whom be glory for ever. Amen."

Chapter 5

SCRIPTURE TESTIMONIES

The value of testimonies upon this subject cannot be questioned. They are entirely Scriptural; and they often bring the Gospel down to the personal level and contact of the sufferer, as mere abstract teaching cannot do. But they should always be simple, modest, as impersonal as possible, and illustrate principles. This is the character of all the Scripture testimonies. We shall glance at a few of these.

THE CASE OF JOB

This is the earliest case fully detailed in the Scriptures.

His sickness came from Satan's touch. His agency in sickness is most distinctly taught by our Lord also, and his power is yet undiminished.

Job's sickness was divinely permitted. It was designed to lead him to search his heart, and see his utter need of sanctification.

His sickness did not sanctify him, but only led to deeper exhibitions of his sin, and self-righteousness. Sickness does not purify anyone, although it may lead us to see our need of holiness and to receive it from God.

His sickness was removed when he saw his sin and acknowledged it before God. This came to him when God revealed Himself. Then he cried: "Now mine eye seeth Thee: wherefore I abhor myself, and repent in dust and ashes." Then came his complete justification, and with it a spirit of forgiveness and love for his enemies. And then, as he prayed for them, the Lord turned his own captivity. When we get right with God, we do not need to pray a great deal for ourselves. As we pray for others, our own blessing will often come. Job's healing made all things new, and all his blessings were doubled. And no doubt the spiritual blessing was the deepest of all.

How instructive to watch this case lying in the hands of God until the soul is ready to learn his spiritual lesson, and then receive from God's own hand life and restoration!

THE WOUNDED ISRAELITES AND THE BRAZEN SERPENT (Num. 21)

This sickness came from sin. They murmured, and God gave them something to murmur for. It is a serious matter to complain, for it is sure to bring the thing we fear, or a worse "I feared a fear, and it came upon me."

This sickness came from Satan; from the serpent. So, still, he stings our life, and poisons our blood. It was a fiery serpent. The Hebrew words are "The serpents, the seraphim." All our spiritual adversaries are not groveling worms. Many of them are lofty and transcendently wise.

The remedy was in the likeness of the disease; in short, a figure of the serpent with the poison extracted, and a striking intimation to the suffering camp and a sin-stricken world that Satan is robbed of his sting, and sickness and sin are but mere shadows of their former selves.

There was also in that brazen serpent the thought of Jesus made for us, Jesus assuming the vile and dishonored name of sinful man, and counted by God, and treated by men, as if He were indeed a serpent and a criminal. Thus for us has He taken the sting from Satan, sin, and death, and hung upon the uplifted cross the trophy of victory.

The healing came by looking at the Brazen Serpent. There is unspeakable power in a look. A look of evil chills the soul. A look of purity and love transfigures it. The eye brings into the soul the object of vision. Looking to the sun, it is present in the eye. Looking unto Jesus brings His life into our whole being.

This was physical life. The same life still comes from the cross for both soul and body, WHILE WE LOOK unto Jesus.

NAAMAN (2 Kings 5)

This was a typical case of disease. Leprosy was the peculiar type of sin, destroying both soul and body. It was the especial stigma of the physical effects of sin.

The instrument of this cure was, in the first instance, a Hebrew maid; and in her great usefulness we learn how God can use a very humble messenger and an incidental word. Indeed, Naaman's own servants, a little later, saved his blessing for him by their wise counsel.

The lesson of humble and Obedient Faith must next be learned. The proud self and will of Naaman must die before his body can be healed by the Divine touch. And so Elisha meets his splendid state with quiet independence, and sends him a simple and humbling message to wash seven times in the Jordan and be clean. The sick are often deeply wounded by our seeming neglect, but God sometimes teaches them thus the lowliness of faith, and takes their thoughts of themselves and others, Naaman, like all other proud sinners, at first refuses the cross, and is about to lose his blessing when a word of honest frankness from his servants brings him to his senses, and sends him to Jordan.

The Faith of Naaman consisted in his doing just what the prophet told him. He took God's way without qualification, and he persevered in it till his blessing came. Perhaps the first or second or sixth time there was no sign of healing; but he pressed on, and at length the wondrous blessing came, the flesh of a little child, and the acknowledgment and sole worship of the great Jehovah he had found.

His request for a gift of earth from the place of his healing was a beautiful foreshadowing of that Earnest of the greater future whom we also receive, the Holy Ghost. The word earnest means a handful of soil. Naaman took home with him a handful of Canaan's soil; and we, in our healing, receive the earnest of the Spirit, a part of Heaven begun on earth.

It is beautiful to see how Elisha sends him away leaning only on God. To his question about bowing in the house of Rimmon, Elisha will give no direct answer, but throws him on God alone, and bids him go in peace. How little man appears in all this! and how simple and glorious is God!

But Satan, too, must have a hand. And he usually shows his hand in some mercenary scheme like Gehazi's. So still, spiritualism and kindred arts of Satan seek to make merchandise of the things of God. But if you look closely, you will see the leper hand and face as white as snow.

HEZEKIAH (2 Kings 28)

It was a hopeless case. All men's reasonings about the part that the remedy had in curing him ought to be set at rest by the fact that he was beyond the reach of every remedy, for even God had said that he should die, and not live. Man and means could, therefore, have nothing to do with his cure; it was wholly Divine.

He turned to God in humility. He made no attempt to find help from man. He threw himself helplessly on the mercy of the Lord. His prayer was not a very trustful one; but God heard his helpless cry, and sent deliverance.

The answer to his prayer was definite and clear. Fifteen years more of life from God Himself. It was sent to Isaiah, and communicated to him; and he at once believed it, and began to praise.

It was accompanied by a double sign. First a reversal of the dial 15 degrees, and then a poultice of figs. Both are called signs. The figs were not medicinal, for medicine was of no avail, but symbolical, and therefore administered by a prophet, not a physician.

The sequel of his healing was unworthy of it. Hezekiah rendered not again according to the benefit, but his heart was lifted up, and long years afterwards the bitter fruits of his sin and folly continued to prove how solemn a thing it is to receive God's great mercies, and how sacredly our redeemed lives must be used for Him. People are always asking, " Did not Hezekiah's case prove the rightness of using remedies?" No. It proved the rightness of doing exactly what God tells us in regard to our healing. God told Naaman to wash in the Jordan. Anything else would have been disobedience. God told Hezekiah to use figs. Anything else would have been disobedience. If God had told us to use figs, anything else would be disobedience. But God has told us to use the anointing oil and the prayer of faith, and is anything else genuine obedience?

THE NOBLEMAN'S SON (John 4)

This was Christ's first miracle of healing. It seems to speak peculiarly to our own times.

It teaches us that we do not need the physical and visible presence of Jesus to heal us. He was far from this sick child and simply spake a word of power, which crossed these intervening spaces with Almighty energy, even as it still can reach from Heaven to earth. "Oh, if He were only here!" you say. Nay, His first great miracle was performed from a distance perhaps as great as between earth and Heaven.

It was by simple, naked faith, without sight or signs. The Lord Jesus had to press this farther away from all but His own simple word, "Except ye see signs and wonders," He exclaimed, "ye will not believe." And then He tested his faith by a simple word, "Go thy way; thy son liveth;" and the man accepted the hard lesson, believed the naked word, and the child was made whole. He showed his faith by quietly going back and ceasing any more to clamor for the Lord's going.

This case began at a fixed moment, and developed quietly and gradually, as so many are now healed. "He inquired at what hour he began to amend." And the answer was that at a certain moment the fever broke. He was now convalescent. So still the dear Master works for all who trust Him. Faith has both its instants and its hours. We must learn to accept both; to count the death-blow struck at the moment of our believing, and then to follow on as it works out all its stages of blessing.

THE HEALING OF PETER'S MOTHER-IN-LAW (Mark 1)

This was Christ's second recorded miracle of healing. He had just come from the Synagogue where, amid the astonishment of the people, He had cast out a demon. Peter's wife's mother was lying sick of fever. It was, then, a case of ordinary disease. And yet our Lord distinctly recognizes another agency at the back of the fever. For "He REBUKED the fever," and this implies some personal and evil agent that must have caused it. He would not rebuke a mere natural law. There is no blame where there is no personal will. Nay, the fever was but the blistering touch of a demon hand; and this was what He rebuked.

Next, she must actively take hold of the healing power which He stands over her to administer. He took her by the hand, and lifted her up, and she arose. There was of course, His mighty touch and Almighty help. But there was also her cooperation, her grasping His extended hand, her shaking off the torpor and weariness of disease, her effort to arise, and her rising. Thus we must meet His help and power.

And then there was the use of her new strength in ministering to Him and them. This was the best proof of healing, the best use of it too. So must we ever give our new life to God, and in ministering to others and forgetting ourselves, we shall find our own strength continually renewed. As we give our life we shall save it; and as we serve others He will administer to all our needs. It is a blessed exchange of responsibility and care to find that we have nothing to do but live for Him, and He but one business, to live for us, and supply all our need.

THE HEALING OF THE MULTITUDE (Matt. 8)

The next cases of healing we read of in the life of Christ were a large number of promiscuous cases on the evening of the Sabbath on which He healed Peter's mother-in-law. They had been gathering all day long, and waiting until the Sabbath was past. And as soon the hour of six o'clock had come, they pressed upon Him from every side, in great numbers and variety, and He healed them all. Now the first lesson we learn from these cases is connected with this very fact, that they waited until the Sabbath was past. It shows how exactly their prevalent ideas of healing resembled the godless ideas of our own secular age. They considered the body, and all that pertained to it, to be purely secular. Healing, therefore, was a mere secular calling, and, as such, unfit work for the holy Sabbath day. Is not this just what modern unbelief has taught the churches of Christendom? The cure of the body is a matter for natural laws and remedies, and secular physicians, a profession to be studied and used for secular profit like any other business, but in no sense as sacred and holy as the salvation and culture of the soul.

For the present our Lord met them on their own ground; but the day soon came when He deliberately and purposely healed on the Sabbath day, that He might repudiate and trample down this absurd and godless idea, and show to men that the body was as sacred as the soul; that its restoration was as much part of God's redemption; that it in no sense was left to be the subject of mere professional treatment; that it was His own holy prerogative and business to heal it; and that it was as holy and sacred work for the Sabbath day as the worship of the Temple or the salvation of the souls of men. The next lesson taught by these cases is the universality of His healing. He healed all that had need. He wished to show that it was not for favorite cases like the mother-in-law of an Apostle, but for all poor, sinful, suffering lives that could trust Him.

And the highest and most helpful of all the lessons is the way in which these cases are linked with the prophecy in Isaiah, announcing the true character of the Messiah as the Bearer of Sickness and Infirmity. It was no mere incidental fact, therefore, that He was healing these sufferers; it was no special and exceptional display of His power as the Son of God. But it was the real purpose and design of His Messiahship; and so all the ages can come to Him and lay upon Him their burdens and pains.

How deep and full these words, "Himself took our infirmities and bare our sicknesses!" Himself, not Himself and physicians, but Himself alone; Himself, not Himself and us, but He takes the whole burden Himself, and leaves us utterly free; Himself, then the healing cannot be had apart from having Him. It is all wrapped up in Himself. His life in us, His indwelling, His body, His flesh; and His bones. Himself took and bare, not merely once, but for ever, not only lifting, but keeping, and carrying for ever. Blessed Healing! Blessed Healer!

THE LEPER (Mark 1)

This occurred soon after, in one of Christ's tours through Galilee.

The request of this man is a good specimen of the state of mind in which we find the average Christian. He has full confidence in the power of Christ to heal, but is very uncertain about His willingness. Now if a friend is going to doubt me at all, I should much rather he would come to me and say, "I am sure you would help me if you could," than "I know you have it in your power to aid me, but I have little confidence in your disposition to do it." When will men see that this easy good-natured talk about God's will involves the MOST SUBTLE AND OFFENSIVE DISTRUST?

Christ's answer to him is explicit and emphatic and ought to settle the question of His will to heal the sincere and trusting sufferer, "I will; be thou clean." There is no evasion or ambiguity, no hesitation or conditioning. It is a great, prompt, kingly answer, and in it all ages may hear His word to us all.

The touch of Christ meant a great deal to a leper. It was a long time since a hand of love had touched him. It was not a cold or mechanical touch. He was moved with compassion. His whole heart of love and his very life were in it. Yes, He helps us, not because His promise compels Him, but with overflowing love and unbounded condescension. He touches our immortal life with His own, and makes our leper hearts quiver with the fresh warm blood of His being.

He must then go to the priest at Jerusalem, and make a proper acknowledgment and testimony, and hold back all other testimony until he has borne witness before the religious authorities of the nation. And so we must bear witness, too, of His mighty works in us, and we must do it where He wants it, perhaps in the very hardest place for us, and IN THE VERY FACE OF RELIGIOUS PRIDE AND OPPOSITION. It was a long journey from Galilee to Jerusalem, but if our testimony requires as great a sacrifice for Him, is not His love worth it all?

THE PARALYTIC (Mark 2)

This is one of the most remarkable of Christ's healing miracles, because He now, for the first time, brought out the doctrine of sin in connection with sickness, and assumed the right on earth to forgive sins. And from this moment He was regarded as a blasphemer. This poor man came for healing, but the Lord saw a deeper need that must first be met. His spiritual life must precede the physical. And so He speaks the word of pardon first. "Son, thy sins be forgiven thee." So we must ever begin. And how many have been led to the very thought of salvation by their need of healing!

Then follows his physical healing. But this, too must be taken by himself in the exercise of bold obedient faith. He was not healed prostrate on that mat. He must rise up, put away his bed, and walk. Christ will not heal you in your bed. You must arise and step out upon His strength.

He was not, as is commonly supposed, healed through the faith of the men who brought him to Jesus, but through his own. Their faith laid him at the feet of Jesus, and brought him the word of forgiving mercy. But his own faith must claim the healing. And it must have been a real faith which could rise up before that throng and carry his bed. The faith of others can do much for us, ADDED to our own, but an unbelieving heart can have nothing from the Lord.

The place of healing, as a token of forgiveness and a sign of Christ's saving power, is very solemn. He did heal this man, that they might know that the Son of man has power on earth to forgive sin. And Christ is ever wanting to convince the world of the reality of His Gospel by His physical miracles. How can we expect men to believe that His spiritual gifts are real when He does not manifest sufficient power to overcome the physical evils of our life? What right has any man to be sure that any part of his religion is real when his faith has never had enough of vigor to accomplish any really difficult thing in his practical life?

THE LAME MAN AT BETHESDA (John 5)

This miracle occurred in Jerusalem about the middle of His ministry. It was His first open and deliberate case of healing on the Sabbath day, and was purposely designed to defy their absurd ideas about the secular nature of disease and healing, and show them that it was sacred enough to be done on the Sabbath day, and to be a part His spiritual ministry. Many people are still afraid of unduly exalting the importance of the body, forgetting that whenever Christ touches it He makes it the channel and the vessel of all holy life and blessing.

The next great lesson of this case has reference to the folly of the things that men depend upon for healing. This man was looking to the fountain of Bethesda to heal him, and had some superstitious idea about its being troubled at times with healing virtues. Now it happens that the verse about the angel stepping in at certain seasons is an interpolation, and that was all a silly lie. So foolish and so false are the hopes of those who look to earthly sources of healing. They disappoint or disappear like Bethesda and its false legend. When the Lord undertook to heal him, He paid no attention to Bethesda or any other means, but spake a single word of power, and bade him go forth in the strength of God.

There is a lesson, too, for the waiting ones who are just hoping for some day of help to come, and go on hoping down to the grave. When Jesus healed him He dispelled all his dreamy future, and started him on the practical and solid ground of a present act of decision. So still hope is often mistaken for faith. The test of faith is that it is always present, and takes the blessing now.

Another most important lesson also is the folly and helplessness of leaning on others. "Sir, I have no man to put me in," expresses the languid dependence of hundreds still who are expecting healing through the help of others, and paralyzing all their own strength and power of believing by looking to some one else's faith and prayers. Others cannot help us until we firmly believe for ourselves. If we cling to them our hands bind and impede them, like the clinging of a drowning man to his rescuer, and both may sink together. But when we have a distinct hold of Christ for ourselves, then He can give our friends a similar grasp for and with us.

Again, "Wilt thou be made whole?" expresses the real element of effectual faith. It acts through a firm and decided will. Faith is not mere will power, but its seat and region is the will. This is the mightiest thing God has given to a man, and no man can receive much from God without a firm and decided choice. We must first see that it is His will to make us whole, and then we must claim it for ourselves with a strength and tenacity which will carry along with it all the power of our being.

Chapter 6

SCRIPTURE TESTIMONIES

One lesson more this poor sufferer must teach us: "Sin no more lest a worse thing come to thee." Not always, yet often, such long and terrible disorders are the direct results of some course of sinful indulgence. Many a life today is impotent because of secret and youthful sin. There must, therefore, be a distinct recognition, confession, and repudiation of all sin, and the redeemed life must be pure and vigilant, if it would retain His sacred life. Each heart and conscience must answer for itself, and God's Spirit will make it very plain to all who desire to know that they may fully obey.

But there is no touchstone so searching as this life of Christ, and there is no cord that binds the soul more sacredly on the Altar of holiness than "I am the Lord that healeth thee." This miracle should not be separated from the discourse which follows on the LIFE which Christ has come to give. It was just an illustration of that blessed life. Christ's healing is neither more nor less than His own Divine life breathed into us, quickening our impotent souls and bodies, and beginning the eternal life now. This is just what He teaches them here. "The Son quickeneth whom He will." "The hour is coming, and NOW IS, when the dead shall hear the voice of the Son of God and they that hear shall live."

THE MAN WITH THE WITHERED HAND (Matt. 12:10)

This miracle was a repetition, in Galilee, of the bold lesson about healing on the Sabbath day, which Jesus had just given in Jerusalem, and healing of the impotent man at Bethesda. They both emphasize the same great principle respecting the freedom of the Sabbath, the sanctity of the body, and the sacredness of its cure.

They both also teach the same great lesson about the necessity of active and aggressive faith in order to receive Christ's healing power. This man was impotent, too, in his diseased hand. He had no power in himself to lift it. But he must, nonetheless, put forth an effort of will and an act of force; not as an attempt either, but in good faith and really expecting to accomplish it. And as he did so, the Divine power quietly and fully met his obedient cooperation, and carried him through into strength and victory.

Thus faith must do the things we have no strength to do, and as it goes forward the new strength will come. The feet must step forward into the deep, and even touch the cold waters as they advance, but He will not fail. In passive waiting there can come no life or power from God. We must put our feet on the soil of Canaan, we must stretch forth our hands and take of the tree of life, and eat, and live forever. The spider taketh hold with her hands, and therefore is in kings' palaces. So many Christians have no hands. They have no grip in their fingers, no stamina in their will, no hold in their faith. Hear His voice, ye listless ones, "STRETCH FORTH THINE HAND."

In his arguments with the Pharisees about this case, Jesus leaves no room to doubt the light in which He regards healing as connected with the will of God. He ridicules their prejudices against His healing a sufferer on the Sabbath, and claims the healing of this man, first on the grounds of simple humanity, as no more than any man would do for an ox or a sheep who had fallen into a pit, and secondly, on the ground of right; to do it is "to do good," "to save life;" not to do it is "to do evil," "to destroy" life. This does not look much like treating sickness as a great boon. And yet such gentle and merciful teachings only exasperated these wicked men; and, when they even see God's power vindicate His teachings, and the man stand forth healed before their eyes, they are filled with madness, and consult how they may destroy Him.

So prejudice still blinds men to the truth and love of God, and as much as ever, today, opposes Christ's healing ministry for the sake of doctrinal consistency.

THE WOMAN WITH THE SPIRIT OF INFIRMITY (Lk. 13:10-20)

This beautiful incident occurred a good deal later, but as it was one of Christ's Sabbath miracles, and comes in the same general class with those just referred to, supplementing and enforcing the same principles, we will introduce it here.

The nature of her disease. It was a case of helpless paralysis and deformity. She was bowed together, and could in no wise lift herself up. It was also of long standing. She had been eighteen years in this condition. It was, therefore, about as difficult a chronic case as could well be brought to the great Healer.

The cause of her disease. Here a ray of marvelously clear and keen light is thrown in not only upon her case, but upon the whole question of disease. The Lord distinctly declares that her troubles had come, not through natural causes, but direct personal agency, the agency of an evil spirit, that her very body is bound by A SPIRIT OF INFIRMITY. And He afterwards declares that SATAN HAS BOUND HER, lo, these eighteen years. He does not recognize it as a case of Providential discipline, but the direct hand of the devil upon her frame. This is incapable of evasion or ambiguity. And it may well make one shudder who has been nursing and petting some foul demon, as if it were an angel.

The question of God's will is also made marvelously clear. There is no greater word in Christian ethics than "OUGHT." It is the word of conscience, of law, of Everlasting Right. It is a cable that binds both God and man. When God says ought, there is no appeal, no compromise, no alternative, nothing but absolutely to obey. It does not mean that a thing is possible, or permissible, or perhaps to be done, but it means that it is necessary to be done and that not to do it would be WRONG. And Christ says to these evil men who would put these petty prejudices before God's beneficent will and His creatures' happiness, "OUGHT NOT THIS WOMAN TO BE LOOSED FROM THIS BOND?" That ought to settle the question of how God regards our healing.

But there is one more principle, the greatest of all, and it conditions and limits this "ought" and everything else in her case; and that is the woman s faith. The Lord expressly calls her a child of faith. That is just the meaning of the expression "a daughter of Abraham." And it is this which makes it a matter of "ought," that she should be healed. "Ought not this woman, being a daughter of Abraham, to be loosed from this bond?" Is it the will of God to heal all? It is the will of God to heal all who believe. More is meant by the expression, "a daughter of Abraham," than mere faith. It expresses a very strong faith, a faith which, like Abraham's, believed without sight, and in the face of seeming impossibilities.

Have we any evidence of such faith on her part? We have. We are told that Jesus called her to Him and said, "Woman, thou art loose from thine infirmity." In the Revised version it is, "He called her." It implies that He required her to come to Him first. This would require supernatural exertion and faith and so she must have made the attempt to come before He touched her. Then, as she came, He declared the work done, "Woman, thou art loosed from thine infirmity;" and He laid his hands upon her and completed the work. But her faith had to take the initiative, and, like Abraham, step out, not knowing whither, on the naked call and strength of God. Then the work could be counted done. "Thou art loosed." And then the full results began to follow.

THE CENTURION'S SERVANT (Matt. 8:5)

The first thing that is remarkable about this case is the high commendation which Christ here gives to the faith of a Gentile and heathen, who possessed so little opportunity of knowing God and enjoying light. The most solemn lesson in all the Bible about faith is that it was most strongly developed in those who had but little light, and the greatest advantages were usually met by the most unreasonable unbelief. They who do not promptly use the light they have are not likely to make a good use of more. This man had very little more light than he had learned from his own profession, and the smattering of Jewish teaching he may have gathered, but he had been a true man as far as he knew his duty, and he had shown his love to God's people and his kindness to the Jewish congregation, whose Synagogue he had built at his own expense.

His strong faith showed itself first in his recognizing Christ's absolute control over all the forces of the universe, even as he controlled his disciplined soldiers; and secondly, in his recognizing the sufficiency of Christ's bare word to stop the disease in a moment. He asked no more than one word from the Lord of Heaven and earth. And that one word he took as a decree as final as the decree of the Caesars. He recognized the authority of Christ's word. It passes over this universe like a great and resistless mandate, and even in the hands of a little child it is as mighty as His own Omnipotence. How tremendous the force of law! Let a single human voice speak the sentence of that Court, and all the power of wealth and influence is helpless to hold back that man from a prison cell. The word which Christ has spoken to us is a word of law, and when faith claims it, all the powers of hell and earth dare not resist it. This is the province of faith, to take that imperial word and use its authority against the forces of disease and sin.

The humility of this man is a beautiful accompaniment of his faith. He deeply felt his unworthiness of Christ's visit. It was not often that a proud Roman acknowledged himself unworthy of a visit, but this Centurion felt that he was standing before One greater than his Emperor, and his spirit bowed in lowly reverence and worship. We can come nearer. Not only will He enter our roof but He will make our heart his home for ever.

THE GADARENE DEMONIACS (Matt. 8:28)

This incident introduces to us a class of cases of great importance, the insane and the disease of the mind. There seems no reason to doubt that they are still the same in character and cause as the instances of demoniacal possession in the days of Christ. The causes of these disorders are distinctly attributed by our Lord to Satanic agency. The power that held this man was sufficient to destroy three thousand swine. What fearful forces one human heart can hold! The power which the evil spirit exerted upon his body, enabling him to break any chain which the hand of man could place upon him, may give us some idea of how spiritual agencies may affect the body either for good or evil. All physical strength is spiritual in its cause. This wretched man seems to have been conscious of two principles within him: one his own will feebly struggling for freedom, the other the evil spirits controlling him, and crushing his will under them. The difference between such a case and one willingly yielded to Satan is very great.

The Lord met this case with deep compassion. He regarded him as the victim of a power he could not resist, and by a word of command He set him free. Immediately his whole appearance was changed. The wild and dreaded maniac is sitting at the feet of Jesus, clothed and in his right mind. The awful power that had possessed him was soon apparent in the destruction of the swine. He himself clung to his Deliverer, and desired to go with Him. But Jesus knew that he needed to be pushed out into the discipline of confession and service, and sent him at once to stand alone and spread the tidings in his home. Every new advance would give him new assurance and strength, and before long the whole region of Decapolis was so stirred by his testimonies, that the way was prepared for the Master's visit and the mighty work which closed with the feeding of the four thousand. So must we often trust the young disciple with the most bold and difficult service and self-reliance.

The treatment of the insane is one of the most important questions connected with the subject of faith. The true remedy is the power of Christ. No doubt it is a subject of much difficulty; and in many cases there are long and severe trials of faith and need for quiet homes where they can be separated, guarded and brought under the influence of Christian teaching and faith. The result of the little that has been attempted has shown how much may be done with holy wisdom and courageous faith.

THE WOMAN WHO TOUCHED HIS GARMENT (Luke 8:48)

The most beautiful thing about this miracle is the way it is embosomed in the heart of a greater, the raising of Jairus' daughter. It would seem as though in these twin miracles the Lord would write, in one striking lesson, the two principles so finely illustrated respectively, in each of God's absolute power on the one hand, even to work where there is nothing but death, and faith's absolute power on the other to take everything from God. They emphasize the two wonderful omnipotences that Christ has linked together: "All things are possible with God," and "all things are possible to him that believeth."

The helpless nature of her disease and the failure of human physicians is brought out with a good deal of plainness of speech. There is no attempt to apologize for the medical profession but we are frankly told that all that had been done for her had only made her worse. It wilt be noticed that it is a physician himself, Luke, who gives us the most vivid picture of all this.

The process of the faith and healing is very striking. There were three stages. First, she believed that she would be healed. She said, "If I may touch his garment, I. shall be whole. Then, secondly, she came and touched. She did something. The personal and living element in faith is here brought out very vividly. Faith is more than believing, it is a living contact with a living Savior. It is the outreaching of a conscious need in us, feeling after and finding its supply in Him. It is not a mere outward approach, not even a mere mental approach. Hundreds thronged Him, but only one TOUCHED Him. Then, thirdly, there is the conscious receiving after the naked believing and the actual coming. Immediately her blood was stanched; she felt in her body that she was whole of her plague. She did not feel first and then believe, but she believed and then she felt.

But her blessing must be confessed. Christ will not allow us to hold his gifts without acknowledgment. Nor can we enjoy and retain them long in secret. Like plants, they need the light of day. And so her womanly sensitiveness must all be laid aside, and her shrinking heart must tell its blessings at His feet, in the hearing of all men. How much we lose by sensitiveness and silence!

And how much she gained by that confession! "Daughter, be of good comfort; thy faith hath made thee whole. Go in peace." A daughter, comforted, healed and now sent forth into peace, that deep, Divine rest that comes with the touch of God, and is the richest part of the inheritance which faith brings. It is not merely that the peace comes into her. She goes into peace, a land so wide and fruitful, that she never can miss its boundaries or exhaust its precious things. And could one little act of faith for her body bring all this deep spiritual blessing? Yes, the most precious part of the blessing His healing gives is that it heals the whole being, and brings us into union with God, with a fullness we never would have known without this living and human touch.

Indeed, it will be found that most of the great spiritual blessings, experiences, and revelations of God to his people in the Scriptures began with what we would call temporal blessings. Abraham became the father of faith by believing in God for a son. Jacob became the Prince of Israel by claiming a temporal deliverance. Daniel saw the coming to Jesus while asking for the Restoration of the Captivity. The Syrophenician woman won her transcendent victory for a suffering child. And so still the things we call little and commonplace, like the little jeweled axles in the wheels of our watches, are the very pivots on which the greatest spiritual experiences turn; and trusting God for a headache or a dollar may teach us to trust Him for all the fullness of His grace and holiness.

THE TWO BLIND MEN (Matt. 9:27)

This little story illustrates several important principles.

Mere prayer will not heal the sick. These blind men followed Him from the house of Jairus crying, "Have mercy on us." And yet it brought no reply. "I have been praying for my healing for forty years," people sometimes say to us, "and I am no better." Well, little wonder, for if you had prayed in faith you would not have prayed so long.

Mere coming into the presence of Christ will not heal us. They came to Him into the house, but still they were not healed. So persons go to meetings, try to get under spiritual influences, and seem to think that those things will bring their blessings. Perhaps they even present themselves definitely to Him for His help and healing, and yet they are no better.

The reason is given in the last step brought out here. All this is of no avail unless we definitely believe that He does do for us what we claim. "Believe ye?" He asks and then utters the great law of faith which determines for every one of us the measure of our blessings, "According to your faith be it unto you." Then His touch brings sight and healing, and they go forth into the glorious light of day.

There is a secret in everything; there is a secret spring or number by which the safe can be unlocked. There is a secret way by which that paper can be brought before the Government. There is a secret by which nature's mighty forces can be harnessed and used. And there is a secret which opens heaven and commands all the forces and resources of the throne. It is not agonizing prayer; it is not much labor; it is simply this: "ACCORDING TO YOUR FAITH BE IT UNTO YOU."

THE SYROPHENICIAN WOMAN (Matt. 15:21)

This was another example of faith where there was little light or opportunity. It is doubtful if this woman had ever heard a promise or a passage of Scripture, or seen an inspired teacher in all her life. She belonged to an alien and accursed race, and everything was against her.

And when she came to Jesus, He seemed against her, too. To her pitiful cry tor help He answered her not a word. To his disciples' appeal to send her away, that is to grant her request and dismiss her, He replies in language which seemed imperatively to exclude her from any right to His mercy. And when at last she came to His very feet and implored His help, He answered in language so harsh and repelling that it seemed like courting insult to approach Him again. He had even called her a dog, the type in the East of that which is unclean and unfit for fellowship and yet in the face of all this her faith only grew the stronger, until at last she drew out of His very refusal the argument for her blessing. Difficulties cannot injure true faith. They are the very stimulus of its growth.

We see the Lord's design in dealing with us, and sometimes seeming to refuse us. All through that struggle He knew and loved her, and saw the trust that would not be denied. And He was but waiting for its full manifestation. Nay, He only tried it because He knew it would stand the trial, and would come forth as gold at last. So He keeps us at His feet, and even seems to refuse our cry, to call forth all the depths of our trust and earnestness. Another object, too, He had with her. He was bringing her to the death of self and the sense of sin. And when at last she was willing to accept His judgment of her, and take her place as a poor worthless sinner, unworthy of any of His blessings, then she could receive all. Faith is a coming down as well as an ascent, a death as well as a life.

Chapter 7

SCRIPTURE TESTIMONIES

Her great faith consisted not only in her persistency, in holding on until the last in importunate pleading, but in its ingenuity in finding some ground on which to plead and claim the blessing. Faith is a process of logic, an arguing our case with God, and it is always looking for something to rest upon. Her heart seemed to lean at first upon His grace and love as she somehow felt it instinctively. Something told her that calm, gentle face could not refuse her. But still she had no word from Him. One little word only, one whisper, one faint concession would do her. But he had spoken nothing but hard, inevitable words of exclusion, exclusion based upon the great principles and limitations of His coming, principles that seemed to make it wrong for Him to help her.

At last He speaks a word that seems to close the door for ever. Not only a Gentile, but a dog. It is NOT MEET. How can she surmount that? Wonderful! That becomes the very bridge on which she crosses the Jordan. A dog -- that gives her a place. A dog -- well, even a dog has some rights. She will claim hers. Only a crumb. This thing she asks is but a crumb to Him, so great that mighty deeds of power and love drop from His fingers like morsels, but oh, so much to her! Lord, I accept it. I lie down at Thy feet, at Thy children's feet; I ask not their fare, but this which is but their leaving; this which will not diminish aught for them; this which even now they in yonder

Galilee have had to the surfeit, until they have refused to take more -- this I humbly claim for myself and child, and Thou canst not say me nay.

No. He could not. Filled with love and wonder, He answers: "Oh woman, great is thy faith; be it unto thee even as thou wilt." And the mighty deed was done. "As thou wilt." Here, again, we have the same element of decision, of fixed and concentrated will which is essential to all strong faith and action. It was the same will, in the negative form, as "I will not" which overcame at Peniel sixteen centuries before; and these two cases, both for a temporal deliverance, are companion pictures of overcoming faith.

THE DEMONIAC CHILD (Matt. 17:14)

Immediately after the Transfiguration, Jesus was brought face to face with the power of Satan in the form of a case of demoniacal possession that resisted all the Disciples. The cause of their failure was their lack of faith, and the reason of their unbelief was their strife about personal ambition.

When Jesus comes to the multitude He rebukes the unbelief which He perceives on every side, and then calls the father and child into his presence. The moment the father begins to speak of the difficulties of the case, he falls into a paroxysm of discouragement and cries, "If Thou canst do anything, have compassion on us, and help us." But the Lord's answer quickly brings him to see that it is not a matter of Christ's power but of his own faith. "If thou canst believe, all things are possible to him that believeth." He at once recognizes the tremendous responsibility which this places upon him, and meets it. "Lord, I believe; help Thou mine unbelief." These two words together -- the Lord's great word to him, and his word to the Lord -- are among the most wonderful teachings of the Bible about faith.

The first tells us the POSSIBILITIES of faith -- all things; equal to God's own omnipotence, for the only one else to whom all things are possible is God. Faith does, indeed, take and use His own Omnipotence.

The second defines the POSSIBILITY of faith -- that is, how far can we believe? Now, many spend their lives wondering if they can believe. Others, more wisely, like this man, put forth the effort and stretch forth the hand first, and then throw themselves on God to sustain and carry them in it. Had he said, "Lord, help my unbelief," without first saying "Lord, I believe," it would have been vain. Had he said, "Lord, I believe;" and stopped there, it would have been equally vain, for it would only have been his own will power. He put forth his will, and then he depended upon Christ for the strength. This is faith. It all comes from Christ, and is, indeed, His own faith in us, but it must be taken by us and used with a firm and resolute hand.

The healing power now comes, but it seems at first only to make matters worse, and develops such a desperate resistance from Satan, that in the conflict the child is thought by the spectators to be really dead. So, often, when God begins to heal us, we really seem to get worse, and the world tells us that we have destroyed ourselves. But the death must precede the life, the demolition the renovation. Let us not fear but trust Him who knows, and all will be well. He takes the child by the hand, and lifts him up, and the demon has left him for ever.

THE BLIND MAN AT BETHSAIDA (Mark 8:22)

The first thing Christ did with this man was to take him by the hand and lead him out of the town, separating him thus from the crowd, giving him time to think, and teaching him to walk. hand in hand with Jesus, and trust Him in the dark. So He first takes us all, and leads us out alone with Himself, long before we look in His face, or know that He is leading us.

Next He begins the work of healing him by a simple anointing, as a sign, and putting His hands upon his eyes. The result is a partial healing, but distorted and unsatisfactory. Thus would He teach us that sometimes our progress will be partial and by successive stages. Many never get beyond this first stage.

There is a third stage -- perfect sight; and it comes from one cause: a look at Jesus. "I see men," he said the first time; and while he only saw men, he saw nothing clearly. But the second time the Lord made Him "look up," and now he saw clearly. That one look at Jesus, even through the dimness, made all things clear and whole.

THE BLIND MAN AT JERUSALEM (John 9)

The question of sin in connection with sickness receives a very important limitation in this incident. Christ teaches His disciples that there are cases of infirmity where there has been no special iniquity beyond the common guilt of all men, and the trouble has been permitted to afford an opportunity for God to show His love and power in restoring.

In the healing of this man, the Lord again used a simple sign. He anointed his eyes with spittle and clay. None will say that this could have any medicinal effect to cure eyes blind from birth. It was simply a sign of His touch. He then sent him to wash in the pool of Siloam, and he came, seeing. If it be said that there was any virtue in the clay, it may be added, with equal force, that he did not receive his sight until the clay had been washed away in the pool of Siloam.

This pool was the type of Christ, and the Holy Spirit, Siloam, was the same as Shiloh, and it meant the Sent One. The water meant the Holy Spirit, also the Sent of the Father and Son.

The testimony of this man, subsequently, was most glorious. With a keen sarcasm, he exposed the inconsistencies of the Scribes and Pharisees who came to see him about it, and to draw out of him some evidence against Christ, who had again broken the Sabbath by this act of healing. But the humble peasant was more than a match for them, and the controversy which follows is intensely sharp and interesting. At last they resort to coarse force, and excommunicate him from the Synagogue. But he is a true martyr; and soon after Jesus appears to him again and reveals His true character and glory, and the man becomes a loving Disciple.

BLIND BARTIMEUS AND HIS COMPANION (Luke 18)

There was a deep insight in the cry of Bartimaeus, "Thou Son of David." Jesus was now coming to claim His throne, and the title by which He was to be known was "The Son of David." It was strange that His own people should be blind to His claim, and that a poor old blind man should be the first to see it. So still the wise are the blind -- so the blind see still.

We see persistent faith. He cried aloud; he cried so much the more when they rebuked him: he cried and threw away his garments, teaching us that we must put all hindrances out of the way. He had but one request: his earnest faith summed up all its intensity in one word, "Lord, that my eyes may be opened." There can be no strong faith without strong desire. The languid prayer has not motive power enough in it to ascend to God.

His healing was simple and glorious. There was a pause, a call, a question, an earnest reply; the word is spoken, the work is done: he gazes on the beautiful scene, the men around him, and the face of the Lord. And then he looks no further, but sends up his shouts of praise, and follows Jesus in the way.

THE WITHERING OF THE FIG TREE (Mark 11:20)

This is Christ's one miracle of judgment, and it would seem to be a poor source of faith and comfort. But Christ made it the occasion of His highest teaching about faith, and it is indeed, a symbol of the deepest and tenderest operation of His Grace. The greatest principle of Scripture is SALVATION BY DESTRUCTION, Life by Death. The life of the world is the destruction of Satan, Sin and Death. The Sanctification of the Soul is the withering up of the natural life. The healing of the body is the death stroke at the root of an evil growth of disease.

There are things that need God's Fire and God's Holiness. There are times when we want more than mercy and gentleness, and the whole spirit longs for the touch of the keen sword which slays utterly the foul thing that is crushing out our life and purity.

Oh, how glorious at such a time is the Consuming Holiness of the Living God? This is the meaning of the withered fig tree. "Ye shall do this which is done to the fig tree," He says to His Disciples. Yes, we can speak that mighty word of faith, and lo, the flesh withers and dies. We can speak it again, and lo, the poison tree of sickness is withered, and begins to dry up from the root. And although leaves and branches may for a while retain their form and color, we know that the death-blow has been struck at the root, and the real work is done.

The secret of all is this: "Have the Faith of God."

The marginal reading is as much higher than the text as heaven is above the earth. The faith of God is as different from faith in God as Christ's faith is from that of the Disciples who were laboring with the demoniac boy. Jesus does mean to teach us that no less than such a faith as His own will do these things, and that we can have it, and must take it.

THE LAME MAN AT THE BEAUTIFUL GATE (Acts 3:10)

The first miracle of the Holy Ghost after Christ's ascension is marked by the most emphatic recognition of THE NAME OF JESUS only as the source of power in its performance, and the most DISTINCT REPUDIATION OF ALL HUMAN POWER OR GLORY IN IT. The Apostles distinctly use that Name as their first word to the man, and when the people come crowding around them, and the rulers summon them before them, they again and again disavow any part in it, further than merely to represent the Mighty Name and power of Him who had been crucified by the men before them. It is not now a present, but an absent Lord, represented by His ministers and His Name.

Again the very faith through which the miracle had been performed and received was as distinctly disavowed, as in any sense their own will-power, or the man's, for they distinctly say, "Yea, THE FAITH WHICH IS BY HIM hath made this man stand before you whole." So that both the faith and the power are SIMPLY JESUS HIMSELF WORKING AND BELIEVING IN US.

Again THE MIRACLE ITSELF IS ONLY VALUED AS A TESTIMONY FOR JESUS, and AN OCCASION FOR MORE WIDELY AND EFFECTUALLY SPREADING HIS WORD. They do not wait to wonder over it. They do not let it monopolize their attention, but they quietly press on with their greater work, the preaching of the Gospel. The healing of the sick is simply accessory to the great and the whole work of the Gospel, and ought always to be associated with it. But the lame man was an unanswerable argument for the Gospel, a very buttress in the walls of the young Church. "Seeing the lame man with Peter and John, they could say nothing against it." That is fine. We need such testimonies still. The world, the infidel, and the devil cannot answer them. We have seen the proudest infidel put to shame by a poor woman coming up before the people who knew her, and telling him how God had made her whole.

ENEAS AT LYDDA (Acts 9:34)

The miracle, by the hands of Peter, has the same features. First, Peter is most careful to recognize only the Master's Power and Name. "Aeneas, Jesus Christ maketh thee whole." Peter is wholly out of sight, and ever must be.

Next, the effect of it is to bring men to God; not to set them wondering, but to set them repenting. All Lydda and Saron saw it, and turned to the Lord. The true effect of a full Gospel of supernatural power and might is always spiritual results, and the salvation of men. And through these mighty signs and wonders will come, Joel tells us, the last great outpouring of the

Spirit upon the world, and the awakening of men before the second coming of the Lord.

THE LAME MAN AT LYSTRA (Acts 14:10)

This is one of the most instructive cases of healing in the Bible.

This was a purely heathen community and audience. They had no preconceived prejudices.

Paul preached to them "the Gospel." No doubt he told them of the healing and redeeming work of Jesus.

As he preached he perceived the light of faith and life irradiating the face of one of his most helpless hearers. We can see these things in men. God gives the spiritual mind instincts of discernment.

Paul evidently would not have gone farther unless he had "perceived" that this man had "faith to be healed." It is no use trying to push men on Christ who have not hands to touch Him. It was not Paul's faith that healed the man, BUT HIS OWN.

But he must be helped to act it out.

"STAND ON THY FEET," cries Paul; and as he rises and attempts in a hobbling, halting way, to stand, he cries "UPRIGHT," for this is the force of the word (see Young's translation). There must be no halting and half-believing. A bold step like this must be carried through audaciously. And lo! the man responds to the brave words, and now not only stands up, but begins to leap and walk. By works his faith is made perfect.

The effect of the miracle and the humble spirit of Paul need no additional word. God was glorified, and Paul gave Him all the glory.

PAUL'S OWN EXPERIENCE OF HEALING (Acts 15:19; 2 Cor. 1:4)

It was not long till the great Apostle had occasion to prove his own faith. The excited people first worshiped and then stoned him and, dragged out of the city by a mob infuriated by Jewish agitators, he was left for dead in the midst of the little band of disciples. But did he die? No. "As the disciples stood round him he rose up in their midst, and the next day he departed for Derbe, and there he preached the Gospel." Could there be anything more simply sublime or sublimely simple? Not a word of explanation, no utterance even of surprise, but a quiet defiance of pain, weakness and death itself, and going on about his work in the strength of the Lord.

In the Second Epistle to the Corinthians and the Fourth Chapter, he gives us the secret of his strength: "We which live are always delivered unto death for Jesus' sake;"--that was what happened at Lystra-" that the life also of Jesus might be made manifest in our mortal flesh." That was the secret of the wondrous restoration at Lystra. In a later verse he gives it to us again, "For which cause we faint not; but though our outward man perish, yet the inward man is renewed day by day."

In the First Chapter of Second Corinthians he gives us another instance of his healing.

It was a great trouble that came to him in Asia, and pressed him out of measure above strength, so that he despaired even of life. And, indeed; when he looked at himself, his condition and his feelings, the only answer he could get was death.

But even in that dark hour he had one confidence, the life of Christ, and "God who raises the dead." And this trust was not in vain. He did deliver from death, and had since been constantly delivering the Apostles, and he was sure would yet deliver him to the end. And he simply adds his thanks to them for the prayers which had so helped and comforted him, and which gave occasion for such wider thanksgiving on his behalf, to the glory and grace of God.

OUR SAVIOR'S EXPERIENCE OF PHYSICAL LIFE IN GOD (Matt. 3)

Jesus Himself had to learn, and leave to us, the great lesson of living physically not on natural strength and support, but on the life of God. This was the very meaning of His first temptation in the wilderness. It was addressed directly to His body. Weakened and worn by abstinence, the tempter came to Him and suggested that He should resort to the usual means of sustenance and strength, and make some earthly bread. The Lord answers him that the very reason of His trial and abstinence is to show that man's life can be sustained without earthly bread, by the life and word of God Himself. The words have a deep significance when we remember that they are quoted from Deuteronomy, and are first used of God's ancient people, to whom, He says, He tried to teach this same lesson, that "Man shall not live by bread alone, but by every word that proceedeth out of the mouth of God."

So it is not only the Son of Man who was thus to live as a special evidence of His Divine power, but the lesson is for man, and we must all learn with Him to receive our life for the body as well as the soul, not by the exclusion of bread, but "not by bread ALONE," but also by God's word. This is exactly what our Savior meant when, two years later, he said in the Synagogue at Capernaum, "As the Living Father hath sent Me, and I live by the Father: so that he that eateth Me even he shall live by Me."

So our Lord learned His physical lesson, refused the Devil's bread, and overcame in His body for us. The next two temptations were addressed to His soul and His spirit, and were, in like manner, overcome. And so He became for us the Author and Finisher of our faith.

Such are some of the witnesses. "Seeing, then, that we are compassed about with so great a cloud of witnesses, let us lay aside every weight, and the sin which doth so easily beset us, and run with patience the race that is set before us, LOOKING UNTO JESUS THE AUTHOR AND FINISHER OF OUR FAITH."

Chapter 8

PERSONAL TESTIMONY

After six years' grateful experience of the Lord's healing in my own life, family and ministry, it may not, be inappropriate to close this little volume with a brief personal testimony.

All that I know of Divine Healing and all that I have written in the preceding pages, the Lord had to teach me Himself in my own life, and I was not permitted to read anything but His own Word on this subject until long after I had learned to trust Him for myself and, indeed, had written much that is in this little book.

For more than twenty years I was a sufferer from many physical infirmities and disabilities. Beginning a life of hard intellectual labor at the age of fourteen I broke hopelessly down with nervous prostration while preparing for college and for many months was not permitted by my physician even to look at a book. During this time I came very near death, and on the verge of eternity gave myself at last to God.

After my college studies were completed I became the ambitious pastor of a large city church at twenty-one, and plunging headlong into my work I again broke down in one year with heart trouble and had to go away for months of rest, returning at length, as it seemed to me at the time, to die. Rallying, however, and slowly recovering in part, I labored on for years with the aid of constant remedies and preventives. I carried a bottle of ammonia in my pocket for years, and would have taken a nervous spasm if I had ventured without it. Again and again, while climbing a slight elevation or going up a stair did the awful and suffocating agony come over me, and the thought of that bottle as a last resort quieted me.

Well do I remember the day in Europe when I ventured to the top of the Righi in Switzerland by rail, and again when I tried to climb the high Campanile stairs in Florence, and as the paroxysm of imminent suffocation swept over me how I resolved that I should never venture into such peril again. God knows how many hundred times in my earlier ministry when preaching in my pulpit or ministering by a grave it seemed that I must fall in the midst of the service or drop into that open grave.

Several years later two other collapses came in my health, of long duration, and again and again during these terrible seasons did it seem that the last drops of life were ebbing out, and a frail thread held the vital chain from snapping forever.

I struggled through my work most of the time and often was considered a hard and successful worker, but my good people always thought me so "delicate," and I grew so weary of being sympathized with every time they met me. Many a neglected visit was apologized for by these good people because I was "not strong." When at last I took the Lord for my Healer I remember I was so tired of this constant pity that I just asked the Lord to make me so well that my people would never sympathize with me again, but that I should be to them a continual wonder through the strength and support of God.

I think He has fulfilled this prayer, for they have often wondered these past six or seven years at the work I have been permitted to do in His name.

It usually took me till Wednesday to get over the effects of the Sabbath sermon, and about Thursday I was ready to begin to get ready for the next Sabbath. Thanks be to God, the first three years after I was healed I preached more than a thousand sermons, and held sometimes more than twenty meetings in one week, and do not remember once feeling exhausted with a single service all the time.

A few months before I took Christ as my Healer, a prominent physician in New York insisted on speaking to me on the subject of my health, and told me that I had not constitutional strength enough left to last more than a few months. He required my taking immediate measures for the preservation of my life and usefulness. During the summer that followed I went for a time to Saratoga Springs, and while there, one Sabbath afternoon, I wandered out to the Indian camp ground, where the jubilee singers were leading the music in an evangelistic service. I was deeply depressed, and all things in life looked dark and withered. Suddenly, I heard the chorus:

> "My Jesus is the Lord of Lords;
> No man can work like Him."

Again and again, in the deep bass notes and the higher tones, that seemed to soar to heaven, they sang it over and over again:

> "No man can work like Him,
> No man can work like Him."

It fell upon me like a spell. It fascinated me. It seemed like a voice from heaven. It possessed my whole being. I took him also to be my Lord of Lords, and to work for me. I knew not how much it all meant; but I took him in the dark, and went forth from that rude, old-fashioned service, remembering nothing else, but strangely lifted up forevermore.

A few weeks later I went with my family to Old Orchard Beach, Ma. I went chiefly to enjoy the delightful air of that loveliest of all ocean beaches. I lived on the very seashore while there, and went occasionally to the meetings on the camp ground, but only once or twice took part in them, and had not, up to that time, committed myself in any full sense to the truth or experience of Divine Healing.

At the same time I had been much interested in it for years. Several years before this I had given myself to the Lord in full consecration, and taken Him for my indwelling righteousness. At that time I had been very much impressed by a remarkable case of healing in my own congregation. I was called to see a dying man given up by all the physicians. I was told that he had not spoken or eaten for days. It was a most aggravated case of paralysis and softening of the brain and so remarkable was his recovery afterwards considered, that it was published in the medical journals as one of the marked cases of medical science.

His mother was a devoted Christian, and he had been converted in his childhood. But now, for many years he had been an actor, and, she feared, a stranger to the Lord. She begged me to pray for him, and as I prayed I was led to ask, not for his healing but that he might recover long enough to let her know that he was saved. I rose from my knees, and was about to leave, and leave my prayer where we too often do, in oblivion, when some of my people called, and I was detained a few minutes introducing them to the mother.

Just then I stepped up to the bed mechanically, and suddenly the young man opened his eyes and began to talk to me. I was astonished and still more so was the dear old mother. And when, as I asked him further, he gave satisfactory evidence of his simple trust in Jesus, I am ashamed to say we were all overwhelmed with astonishment and joy. From that hour he rapidly recovered, and lived for years. He afterwards called to see me, and told me that he regarded his healing as a miracle of Divine power. The impression produced by this incident never left my heart.

Soon afterwards I attempted to take the Lord as my Healer, and for awhile, as long as I trusted Him, He sustained me wonderfully, but afterwards, being entirely without instruction and advised by a devout Christian physician that it was presumption, I abandoned my position of simple dependence upon God alone, and so floundered and stumbled for years. But as I heard of isolated cases I never dared to doubt them, or question that God did sometimes so heal. For myself, however, the truth had no really practical or effectual power, for I never could feel that I had any clear authority in a given case of need to trust myself to Him.

But the summer I speak of I heard a great number of people testify that they had been healed by simply trusting the Word of Christ, just as they would for their salvation. It drove me to my Bible. I determined that I must settle this matter one way or the other. I am so glad I did not go to man. At His feet, alone, with my Bible open, and with no one to help or guide me, I became convinced that this was part of Christ's glorious Gospel for a sinful and suffering world, and the purchase of His blessed Cross, for all who would believe and receive His Word. That was enough.

I could not believe this and then refuse to take it for myself, for I felt that I dare not hold any truth in God's Word as a mere theory or teach to others what I had not personally proved. And so one Friday afternoon at the hour of three o'clock, I went out into the silent pine woods, I remember the very spot, and there I raised my right hand to Heaven and in view of the Judgment Day, I made to God, as if I had seen Him there before me face to face, these three great and eternal pledges:

As I shall meet Thee in that day, I solemnly accept this truth as part of thy Word, and of the Gospel of Christ and, God helping me, I shall never question it until I meet Thee there.

As I shall meet Thee in that day I take the Lord Jesus as my physical life, for all the needs of my body until all my lifework is done; and God helping me, I shall never doubt that He does so become my life and strength from this moment, and will keep me under all circumstances until His blessed coming, and until all His will for me is perfectly fulfilled.

As I shall meet Thee in that day I solemnly agree to use this blessing for the glory of God, and the good of others and to speak of it or minister in connection with it in any way in which God may call me or others may need me in the future.

I arose. It had only been a few moments, but I knew that something was done. Every fibre of my soul was tingling with a sense of God's presence. I do not know whether my body felt better or not -- I know I did not care or want to feel it -- it was so glorious to believe it simply, and to know that henceforth He had it in hand.

Then came the test of faith. The first struck me before I had left the spot. A subtle voice whispered: "Now you have decided to take God as your healer, it would help if you should just go down to Dr. Cullis' cottage and get him to pray with you." I listened to it for a moment without really thinking. The next, a blow seemed to strike my brain, which made me reel for a moment as a man stunned. I staggered and cried: "Lord, what have I done?" I felt I was in some great peril. In a moment the thought came very quickly, "That would have been all right before this, but you have just settled this matter forever, and told God you will never doubt that it is done."

I saw it like a flash of lightning, and in that moment I understood what faith meant, and what a solemn and awful thing it was inexorably and exactly to keep faith with God. I have often thanked God for that blow. I saw that when a thing was settled with God, it was never to be unsettled. When it was done, it was never to be undone or done over again in any sense that could involve a doubt of the finality of the committal already made. I think in the early days of the work of faith to which God afterwards called me, I was as much helped by A HOLY FEAR OF DOUBTING GOD as by any of the joys and raptures of His presence or promises. This little word often shone like a living fire in my Bible: "IF ANY MAN DRAW BACK, MY SOUL SHALL HAVE NO PLEASURE IN HIM." What the enemy desired was to get some element of doubt about the certainty and completeness of the transaction just closed, and God mercifully held me back from it.

The next day I started to the mountains of New Hampshire. The next test came on the following Sabbath, just two days after I had claimed my healing. I was invited to preach in the Congregational Church. I felt the Holy Spirit pressing me to give a special testimony. But I tried to preach a good sermon of my own choosing. It was about the Holy Ghost, and had often been blessed, but it was not His word for that hour, I am sure.

He wanted me to tell the people what He had been showing me. But I tried to be conventional and respectable, and I had an awful time. My jaws seemed like lumps of lead, and my lips would scarcely move. I got through as soon as I could, and fled into an adjoining field, where I lay before the Lord and asked Him to show me what my burden meant and to forgive me. He did most graciously, and let me have one more chance to testify for Him and glorify Him.

That night we had a service in our hotel, and I was permitted to speak again. This time I did tell what God had been doing. Not very much did I say, but I tried to be faithful in a stammering way, and told the people how I had lately seen the Lord Jesus and His blessed Gospel in a deeper fullness, as the Healer of the body, and had taken him for myself, and knew that He would be faithful and sufficient. God did not ask me to testify of my feelings or experiences, but of Jesus and His faithfulness. And I am sure He calls all who trust Him to testify before they experience His full blessing. I believe I should have lost my healing if I had waited until I felt it.

I have since known hundreds to fail just at this point. God made me commit myself to Him and His healing covenant, before He would fully bless me. I know a dear brother in the ministry, now much used in the Gospel and in the Gospel of Healing, who received a wonderful manifestation of God's power in his body and then went home to his church but said nothing about it, and waited to see how it all held out. In a few weeks he was worse than ever, and when I met him next time he wore the most dejected face you could imagine. I told him his error, and it all flashed upon him immediately. He went home and GAVE GOD THE GLORY for what He had done, and in a little while his church was the center of a blessed work of grace and healing that reached far and wide and he himself was rejoicing in the fullness of Jesus.

I am very sure that Sabbath evening testimony did me more good than anybody else, and I believe that if I had withheld it I should not now be writing the pages of the Gospel of Healing. Well, the next day the third test came.

Nearby was a mountain 3,000 feet high -- I was asked to join a little party that were to ascend it. I shrank back at once. Did I not remember the dread of heights that had always overshadowed me, and the terror with which I had resolved in Switzerland and Florence never to attempt it again? Did I not know how an ordinary stair exhausted me and distressed my poor heart?

Then came the solemn searching thought, "If you fear or refuse to go, it is because you do not believe that God has healed you. If you have taken Him for your strength, need you fear to do anything to which He calls you?"

I felt it was God's thought. I felt my fear would be, in this case, pure unbelief, and I told God that in His strength I would go.

Just here I would say that I do not wish to imply that we should ever do things just to show how strong we are, or without any real necessity for them. I do not believe that God wants His children needlessly to climb mountains or walk miles just because they are asked to. But in this case, and there are such cases in every experience, I needed to step out and claim my victory sometime, and this was God's time and way. He will call and show each one for themselves. And whenever we are shrinking through fear He will be very likely to call us to the very thing that is necessary for us to do to overcome the fear.

And so I ascended that mountain. At first it seemed as if it would almost take my last breath. I felt all the old weakness and physical dread; I found I had in myself no more strength than ever. But over against my weakness and suffering I became conscious that there was another Presence. There was a Divine strength reached out to me if I would have it, take it, claim it, hold it, and persevere in it. On one side there seemed to press upon me a weight of Death, on the other an Infinite Life. And I became overwhelmed with the one, or uplifted with the other, just as I shrank or pressed forward, just as I feared or trusted; I seemed to walk between them and the one that I touched possessed me. The wolf and the Shepherd walked on either side, but the Blessed Shepherd did not let me turn away. I pressed closer, closer, closer, to His bosom and every step seemed stronger until when I reached that mountain top, I seemed to be at the gate of Heaven, and the world of weakness and fear was lying at my feet. Thank God, from that time I have had a new heart in this breast, literally as well as spiritually, and Christ has been its glorious life.

A few weeks later I returned to my work in this city, and with deep gratitude to God I can truly say, hundreds being my witnesses, that for nearly seven years I have been permitted to labor for the dear Lord in summer's heat or winter's cold without interruption, without a single season of protracted rest, and with increasing comfort, strength and delight. Life has had for me a zest, and labor an exhilaration that I never knew in the freshest days of my childhood.

The Lord has permitted the test to be a very severe one. A few months after my healing He called me into the special pastoral, evangelistic and literary work which has since engaged my time and energy, and which I may truthfully say has involved fourfold more labor than any previous period of my life.

Besides the evangelistic and pastoral work of my church, involving most of this time, several sermons every week, there have been the following additional labors: the entire editorial charge and much of the writing of a monthly magazine; the preparation of several tracts and volumes; the personal supervision of the entire publishing work and the responsibility for a large correspondence; the oversight of Berachah Home, with the reception every week of many callers and inquirers, and several meetings there; one or two lectures daily during seven months in the year at the Missionary Training College, requiring the most elaborate and careful thought; and many meetings and conventions in various places with God's dear children.

Much of this work has had to be done at night, and through long protracted exertion covering often from twelve to sixteen or even eighteen hours of labor in the twenty-four. And yet I desire to record my testimony to the honor and glory of Christ, that it has been a continual delight and seldom any burden or fatigue, and much, very much easier in every way than the far lighter tasks of former years.

I have been conscious, however, all the time that I was not using my own natural strength. Physically I do not think I am any more robust than ever. I would not dare to attempt for a single week what I am now doing on my own constitutional resources. I am intensely conscious with every breath, that I am drawing my vitality from a directly supernatural source, and that it keeps pace with the calls and necessities of my work. Hence, on a day of double labor I will often be conscious at the close of double vigor, and feel just like beginning over again, and indeed almost reluctant to have even sleep place its gentle arrest on the delightful privilege of service. Nor is this a paroxysm of excitement to be followed by a reaction, for the next day comes with equal freshness, and all this has gone on for nearly seven years, and they following close on a worn out constitution, and twenty years of suffering.

I have noticed this, that my work is easier and seems to draw less upon my vital energy than before. I do not seem to be using up my own life in the work now, but working on a surplusage of vitality supplied by another source. I believe and am sure that is nothing else than "the life of Christ manifested in my mortal flesh." Once or twice since I took the Lord for my strength I have felt so wondrously well that I think I began to rejoice and trust in the God-given strength. In a moment I felt it was about to fail me, and the Lord instantly compelled me to look to HIM, as my continual strength, and not even depend upon the strength He had already given.

I have found many other dear friends compelled to learn this lesson and suffering until they fully learned it. It is a life of constant dependence on Christ physically as well as spiritually. One night, especially, I remember returning from a distant city and finding at a late hour several hours of night work on my desk that it seemed necessary to do before morning. In myself I felt at the moment physically unable to do it, and heart and brain both seemed to tremble at the sight. But I looked to God and became fully assured that it was His Work and His Will that I should do it then. I took up my pen, and in a few hours it was joyfully finished, and when it was done, instead of being exhausted I was fresher than when I rose in the morning and ready to lie down with tranquil nerves and sleep as peacefully as a child.

I know not how to account for this, unless it be the imparted life of the dear Lord Jesus in my body. I am surely most unworthy of such an honor and privilege, but I believe He is pleased in His great condescension to unite Himself with our bodies, and I am persuaded that His body, which is perfectly human and real, can somehow share its vital elements with our organic life, and quicken us from His Living Heart and indwelling Spirit.

I have learned much from the fact that Samson's physical strength was through "the Spirit of the Lord," and that Paul declares that although daily delivered to death for Jesus' sake, yet the very life of Christ is made manifest in his body. I find that "the body is for the Lord, and the Lord for the body," that "our bodies are members of Christ," and that "we are members of His body, His flesh and His bones. I do not desire to provoke argument, but I give my simple, humble testimony and to me it is very real and very wonderful. I know "it is the Lord." I know many of my brethren who have entered into the same blessed experience. I only want to consecrate and use it more and more for Him. I feel what a sacred and holy trust it is. And I so wish that my weary, broken-down and overladen brethren could but taste its exquisite joy and its all-sufficient strength.

I would like to add, for my brethren in the ministry, that I have found the same Divine help for my mind and brain as for my body. Having much writing and speaking to do, I have given my pen and my tongue to Christ to possess and use, and He has so helped me that my literary work has never been a labor. He has enabled me to think much more rapidly and to accomplish much more work, and with greater facility than ever before. It is very simple and humble work, but such as it is it is all through Him, and I trust for Him only. And I believe, with all its simplicity, it has been more used to help His children and glorify His name than all the elaborate preparation and toil of the weary years that went before.

TO HIM BE ALL THE PRAISE.

Chapter 9

TESTIMONY OF THE WORK

I desire to add a few words about the origin of the work in connection with Divine Healing in this city, and some of the cases that I have known.

As I have already stated in the former chapter, one of the pledges I made to the Lord in connection with my own healing was that I would use this truth and my experience of it for the good of others, as He should require and lead me.

This meant a good deal for me, for I had a great deal of conservative respectability and regard for my ecclesiastical reputation to die to. I knew intuitively what it might cost to be wholly true in this matter, and at the same time I shrank unutterably from the thought of having to pray with any one else for healing. I feared so much that I should involve God's name in dishonor by claiming what might not come to pass, and I almost hoped that I might not have to minister personally in this matter, and was intensely glad that there were other brethren whom God had already raised up for this work and I should gladly strengthen their hands.

My first public testimony to the truth in this city, made in the course of a sermon to my own people, then a Presbyterian Church in New York, awakened little or no opposition. A few weeks later I was asked to speak at the Anniversary of the Fulton Street Prayer Meeting, the day of President Garfield's funeral. The Lord led me to speak frankly, and refer to the true scriptural method of prayer for the healing of the sick directly in the name of the Lord Jesus. At the close of my address there was but one to give me a word of response, and that was a good old Presiding Elder of the Methodist Episcopal Church, who has since gone to his rest. He thanked me very cordially and said he believed every word I had said.

Soon after the test came in my own family. My little girl became suddenly very ill with diphtheria. Her mother, not then believing at all as I did insisted upon having a physician, and was much distressed when I simply took the little one to God and claimed her healing in the name of the Lord Jesus. That night, with a throat as white as snow and a raging fever the little sufferer lay beside me alone. I knew that if the sickness lasted to the following day there would be crisis in my family, and I should be held responsible. The dear Lord knew it, too. With trembling hand I anointed the brow, it was the first or second person I ever anointed and claimed the power of Jesus' name. About midnight my heart was deeply burdened. I cried to God for speedy deliverance. In the morning her throat was well, and the mother, as she came to see the sick one, gave me one look, when she saw the ulcers gone and the child ready to get up and go about her play, which I shall never forget. From that hour I was never again asked to get a physician in my home. And God has wondrously cared for the little ones. They have hardly known sickness, and as often as it has come, the Lord has Himself removed it, except where some lesson was to be learned, and then the place of the true penitence has always brought restoration and deliverance.

About this time, the Lord led me to commence the special work of faith which has since engaged my life. This was not by any means to teach Divine healing, but to preach the Gospel to the neglected masses by public evangelistic and free services. For several years no single word about bodily healing was spoken in these meetings, our supreme object being to lead men to Christ, and not prejudice them by any side issues. But the facts about my own healing and the healing of my child got abroad quietly about my little flock, and one and another came to me to ask about it, and whether they could not be healed also. I told them they could if they would believe, as I had done, and I sent them to their homes to read God's Word for themselves and ponder and pray.

The first of them was a dear sister, then widely known in Christian work, who afterwards became a deaconess in our home. She had been for twenty years a sufferer from heart disease. She took about a month to weigh the matter, and then in her calm, decided way came to have her case presented to God. She was instantly healed, and for several years worked untiringly, and hardly knew what weariness even meant. At length she finished her work and fell asleep, amid great peace and blessing.

One and another now began to come and ask about it, and, at length, the Friday meeting grew up as a place and time where all who were interested in this special theme could come together and be instructed and strengthen each other by mutual testimony. This meeting has since grown to be a gathering of several hundred people from all the evangelical churches and many different homes.

The cases of healing that have come under my notice in these years would fill many volumes. They have represented all social extremes, all religious opinions, all professions and callings, and all classes of disease. I have had spiritualists come, broken down at length by the service of Satan and seeking deliverance from their sufferings -- but I have never felt free even to pray with such cases without a complete renunciation of this terrific snare. I have had some sad and shameful disclosures of its evils. I have had Roman Catholics also come as if they were consulting some superstitious rite. And sometimes when they have been patiently instructed and led to the true Savior, I have seen them healed. I have had men come and offer large sums if they or their dear ones could be prayed well, but I have never dared to touch such cases except to send them directly to Christ, and tell them that at His feet only, in true penitence and trust could they expect deliverance.

I have had poor sinners come seeking healing, and go having found salvation. Many persons have been led to Christ through their desire to escape disease. I have never felt that I could claim the healing of any one until they first accepted Jesus as a Savior. But I have several times seen the soul saved and the body healed in the same hour. I have never allowed any one to look to me as a healer, and have had no liberty to pray for anyone while they placed the least trust in either me or my prayers, or aught but the merits, promises and intercessions of Christ alone.

My most important work has usually been to get myself and my shadow out of people's way, and set Jesus fully in their view. I have seen very humble and illiterate Christians suddenly and gloriously healed and baptized with the most wonderful faith, and I have seen brilliant intellects and Christians who had great reputations unable to touch even the border of His garment. Usually they could not get low down enough to do this. I saw a brilliant physician once rise in the meeting and make a learned speech about it, and I saw a humble girl who when I first met her did not seem to have capacity enough to grasp the idea, healed by his side of the worst stage of consumption, and her shortened limb lengthened two inches in a moment. I have seen this blessed gift of Christ bring relief and unspeakable blessing to the homes of many of the poor, and take from worn and weary working women a bondage like Egypt's iron furnace.

And I have also seen it enter the homes of many of the refined, the cultivated, and the wealthy who have not been ashamed to witness a good confession and bear a noble testimony to Christ as a complete Savior. I have seen the theologian often answered after his most logical assaults upon it, by the healing of some of his own people in a way he could not answer or explain. Sometimes I have taken one of these simple cases to a boasting infidel and asked her to tell him her simple story, and he has been overwhelmed, silenced and sometimes departed deeply impressed. One of the most brilliant lawyers in this city told me that he was fully convinced of the truth of Christianity quite recently by the healing of our good friend, John Elsey, and the consecrated life that has followed it.

Often have I had women of the world broken down under deep conviction of sin, and brought to seek a deep and true religious life by the real and simple testimonies of the Friday meeting. I have seen many beloved ministers accept the Lord Jesus in His fullness for soul and body, and some of the most devoted and distinguished servants of Christ in this city are proud to own Him as their Healer.

But I have also noticed that the ecclesiastical strait-jacket is the hardest fetter of all, and the fear of conservative and ecclesiastical opinion the most inexorable of all bondage. Not a few beloved physicians of the highest standing have taken Jesus as their Healer and when their patients are prepared for it, love to lead them to His care. Several of these can be seen at our Friday meeting, and many of them are to be met within other cities. Many of the most consecrated Christian workers and city missionaries have found this precious truth, and some have had a bitter ordeal of prejudice and opposition to face in their churches and societies, but where they have been wise, true and faithful God has vindicated them in the end.

I have found that the most spiritually minded men and women in the various churches are usually led to see and receive this truth. WHEN CHRIST BECOMES AN INDWELLING AND PERSONAL REALITY IN THE SOUL, IT IS HARD TO KEEP HIM OUT OF THE BODY. I have not found any serious practical difficulty in dealing with the question of remedies. Where one sets any value upon them or is not himself clearly led of the Lord to abandon them, I never have advised him to do so. There is no use in giving up remedies without a real faith in Christ. And where one really commits his case to Christ and believes that he has undertaken it, he does not want, as a rule, to have any other hand touch it, or indeed see that anything else is necessary. Where persons have real faith in Christ's supernatural help they will not want remedies. And where they have not this faith, I have never dared to hinder them from having the best help they can obtain.

I have never felt called to urge any one to accept Divine Healing. I have found it better to present the truth and let God lead them. Often when urging them most strongly not to attempt it unless they were fully persuaded, the effect has been to impel them to it more strongly and to show that they had real faith. I have never felt that Divine Healing should be regarded as the Gospel. It is part of it, but we labor much more assiduously for the salvation and sanctification of the souls of men. The secular press, with its love of the sensational, has tried to present this doctrine as a special hobby on the part of some of us, but in reality we have but one public service in the week for this, and seven for spiritual instruction and blessing.

The cases of healing have been very various. One of the most remarkable in the early days was a woman who had not bent her joints for eight years, and used to stand in our meetings on her crutches, unable to sit down during the whole service. She had not sat for eight years. She was healed in a moment, as if by the touch of a feather, and all in the house were filled with wonder. Another was cured of spinal curvature. A great many have been delivered from fibroid tumors; and a few cases from malignant and incurable cancers. We have had two cases of broken bones restored without surgical aid. Many cases of the worst forms of heart disease, several of consumption, and some desperate cases of hernia, when it would have been death to walk forth as they did if Christ had not sustained. Paralysis and softening of the brain, epilepsy and St. Vitus' dance, have all been markedly cured, and a few cases of dangerous insanity have also been restored through believing prayer. The numbers of such cases will reach to thousands. To give even a few in detail would be impossible.

That which has been our chief joy is that the fruits are so blessed and glorious in the consecrated lives that have thus been redeemed from destruction and given to the work of God and the needs of men. One of the dear ones is in charge of a mission where hundreds are led to Christ. Another, refused by her Board on account of illness, was healed by the Lord and is now again in India with her husband, preaching Christ to the heathen. Some are in Japan, some in Africa, some in South America, some in England, and many in the streets and lanes of the city, and in the most earnest work of the land. God be thanked for the blessings they have received, and the blessings they have become.

During these years God has opened our Berachah home and allowed us to meet hundreds of His dear children within its walls, and see them go forth in strength and blessing. Other homes are scattered over this and other lands, and already a great multitude in this and other lands are joining hands and singing together as they journey home.

"Bless the Lord, 0 my soul, and forget not all His benefits. Bless the Lord, 0 my soul, and all that is within me bless His Holy name, who forgives all your iniquities, who heals all your diseases, who redeems your life from destruction, who crowns you with loving kindness and tender mercies, who satisfies your mouth with good things, so that your youth is renewed like the eagles."

Appendix

CHRISTIAN SCIENCE, SO-CALLED

Many persons strangely confound this strange anti-Christian error with Divine Healing, and many who ought to know better are insiduously drawn into its snare by the numerous superficial tracts and publications which it circulates, making no reference to its real teachings and infidel philosophy and containing only a few simple and seemingly harmless directions about ignoring symptoms, etc. We therefore add from our own and other volumes a few careful statements of its real character, with direct quotations from its own standard authorities This philosophy denies that Jesus Christ has come in the flesh. It denies the reality of Christ's body; therefore, it is anti-Christian in its teaching. This is not divine healing. There is no fellowship between the two. It is one of the delusions of science, falsely so called. It would undermine Christianity. It is the most fatal infidelity. It does away entirely with the atonement, for as there is no sin there can be no redemption. I would rather be sick all my life with every form of physical torment, than be healed by such a lie.

Much of it is vague and confusing, but wherever doctrines and principles are clearly stated, they are utterly antagonistic to the Scriptures. It is a little like Buddhism, as has been said by some one before but much like English Deism and Idealism, combined with German Pantheism. It denies explicitly the existence of matter, the creation of the material universe by God, the atonement of Jesus Christ, and the distinctive doctrines of the Christian system. It propounds a series of principles, some of which we quote from Mrs. Edey's standard book:

PLATFORM OF CHRISTIAN SCIENTISTS

1. That there is neither a personal Deity, a personal Devil, nor a personal man.

2. That God is Principle and not person, Mind and not Matter : that this principle is what the Scripture declares it, namely, Life, Truth and Love.

3. That God, which is the perfect Mind or Principle, including the perfect idea, is all that is real or eternal.

5. That Spirit is the only substance, even "the substance of things hoped for and the evidence of things not seen." The spiritual and eternal are substance, whereas the material and temporal are not substance.

10. That man was and is the idea of God, the conception of Mind; that this idea was co-existent and co-eternal with Mind; hence, that man was forever In Mind, but Mind was never in man. There was never a material idea or personal man. All is mind, there is no matter; all is harmony, there is no discord; all is Life, there is no death; all is good, there is no evil; all is God and His idea.

11. That Science decides matter or the mortal body to be nothing but a belief and an illusion. If you besiege sickness, sin or death with this scientific understanding of being, you will learn that our statement of God and man is true, and the opposite statement of them is the error and discord that Truth casts out. . . . As the mythology of Pagan Rome has yielded to a more spiritual idea of Deity, so shall our material theology or doctrinal religions yield to a more spiritual idea of God than a material man presents, until all materiality shall disappear in thought, and the finite give place to the infinite, and the imper-

sonal, unlimited and unerring idea, and the impersonal, limitless or infinite Principle of this idea shall appear, and "Thy kingdom have been on earth as it is in Heaven."

13. There is but one Spirit or God, hence there are no spirits or gods, and no evil spirit, because Spirit is God. A personal God, a personal man, a personal devil, and evil and good spirits, are theological mythoplasm, mere beliefs that must finally yield to the opposite science of God and man.

18. That Life; Truth and Love are the Trinity, or Triune Principle, the three in one, the same in action and entity, and these are the one God. That the Holy Ghost is divine science, revealing and explaining this triune principle, and leading into all Truth; that Christ is but another term for God, and Jesus was the name of a man. The conception of Jesus was spiritual. The spirituality of Mary was the transparency through which immortal Mind was reflected in that better likeness of Truth and Love, the good and pure Jesus. Into Mary's idea of God and conception of man, the male, or sensual element of thought entered not to taint the idea; thus it was that Jesus became the mediating or intervening idea between Truth and error, of soul and sense, which opposed not God, that healed the sick, dispelled the illusions of sense, or the belief of Life and Intelligence in matter, and revealed the impersonal Truth, namely, that soul and God are one, and the "I" or the Father.

19. That our church is built on Christ, not a person, but the Principle that Christ said "is the Way, the Truth, and the Life;" that Christian Science is the Way, and its foundations are eternal.'"

Dr. Gordon, of Boston, thus sums up its teachings: Christian Science calls itself "the understanding of God," which is simply the translation of the Greek word "theosophy." One of the fundamental axioms of theosophy is set forth in the following sentence: "There is no personal devil. That which is mystically called the devil is the negative and opposite of God. And whereas God is I AM, or positive Being, the devil is not." Its platform opens with the astounding declaration "that there is neither a personal Deity, a personal devil, nor a personal man."

Beyond its palpable contradictions of the Word of God, we must confess also the shock which it gives to our reverence to hear Jesus constantly spoken of as a metaphysician and demonstrator of Christian Science--"the most scientific Man that ever trod the globe;" to be told that the cause of His agony in the garden was that He was touched with "the utter error of a belief of life in matter;" that on the cross He was giving this world "an example and proof of Divine science;" that His Christianity "destroyed sin, sickness and death, because it was metaphysics and personal sense, bore the cross and reached the right hand of a perfect Principle."

It will hardly be necessary, after what has been said, to distinguish "Christian Science" from the "prayer of faith," which is said in the Scripture to "save the sick." No one who believes this promise or makes use of it, has ever, so far as we know, considered that its fulfillment depends on the action of mind upon mind. All who credit "faith cures," as they are sometimes called, hold that they are the result of God's direct and supernatural action upon the body of the sufferer. "Christian Science" pointedly denies the efficacy of prayer for the recovery of the sick. It says:

"Asking God to heal the sick has no effect to gain the ear of love, beyond its ever presence. The only beneficial effect it has is mind acting on the body through a stronger faith to heal it; but this is one belief casting out another-a belief in a personal God casting out a belief in sickness, and not giving the understanding of the principle that heals"- (Science and Health, It., 171).

Here the antagonism between two things that differ is so marked that we only aced call attention to it.

Rev. Green Wood, of Chicago, adds these forcible words: "The chief cornerstone of science is the following postulate: That the immortal basis of Life is soul, not body, Life, not death," i.e. the immortal basis of Life is Life, or Life is its own basis. But enough. This seems very like a mouse racing around in a peck measure in pursuit of his own tail. Is not this the baseless fabric of a vision?

Is not this the necromancy for resort to which Saul, King of Israel, lost his Kingdom and his life, and the penalty for which, under the Theocracy, was death? Is not this the Gnostic mysticism of the first century which claimed that the body of our Lord Jesus Christ was a myth, or as now set forth, an idea? To meet this Gnostic mysticism, John wrote his first epistle, wherein he sets forth, by Divine authority, that the man Jesus was not a myth, not an "idea," but a veritable person-a real man. See I John 4:2, 3: "Hereby know ye the Spirit of God. Every spirit that confesseth that Jesus Christ is come in the flesh is of God, and every spirit that confesseth not that Jesus Christ is come in the flesh is not of God. And this is that spirit of Antichrist whereof ye have heard that it should come, and even now already is in the world."

Chap. 5:1: Jesus is the Son of God. "Little children, keep yourselves from idols." At the last, false Christs and false prophets shall arise, and shall show signs and wonders to seduce if possible even the elect. But take ye heed. Behold I have foretold you all things. Let all beware, lest following after this *ignis fatuus* they thereby prove themselves to be not of the elect, but the dupes of Buddhism and Gnostic mysticism insidiously palmed off upon Christian America in this nineteenth century under the guise of "Christian Science"!

www.ingramcontent.com/pod-product-compliance
Lightning Source LLC
Chambersburg PA
CBHW020422010526
44118CB00010B/384